A LIFE WORTH LIVING

A LIFE WORTH LIVING

BY
LESA TACON

Nenge Books, Australia

A Life Worth Living
by Lesa Tacon

Text and photos copyright © Lesa Tacon 2022
All rights reserved.

Without limiting rights under the copyright above, no part of this publication shall be reproduced, stored in or introduced into a retrieval system, or transmitted in any form and by any means (electronic, mechanical, photocopy, recording or otherwise) without the prior written permission of the publisher. Permission is granted for exerpts from this book to be used in Christian education and ministry contexts provided the following copyright acknowledgement is included:

'Excerpted from "A Life Worth Living", copyright © Lesa Tacon 2022, published by Nenge Books, www.nengebooks.com'.

Published by Nenge Books, Australia, June 2022.
www.nengebooks.com
nengebooks1@gmail.com
Design and desktop by Nenge Books.

Nenge Books publishes quality books using print-on-demand (PoD) technology to enable independent authors to publish, both small and large print runs. Author enquiries are welcome at nengebooks1@gmail.com. This book can be purchased online at www.nengebooks.com.

ISBN 978-0-6488889-7-0

For Oliver, Sayla, Ellie and Miles.

I pray that you will learn to trust God throughout your lives in all that you do. He loves you and knows each of you and has a purpose and plan for your lives to do great things. This part of my story is to encourage you to go for it. Nothing is impossible when you walk with Jesus.

CONTENTS

Foreword	ix
Introduction	xi
Acknowledgements	xiii
1. Calling	1
2. Culture Shock!	6
3. Taking back ground and opportunities arise	11
4. Survival of the fittest	15
5. Healing Broken Hearts	18
6. Destiny	22
7. Beginnings	25
8. Small Fire – Large Flame	31
9. Divine connections	35
10. Beautiful Women	45
11. Lost in Translation	53
12. Babies and Jjajas	56
13. We are slow but we are sure!	60
14. Teaching and Child Sacrifice	65
15. Adventure is risk	69
16. Jiggers and other delights	73

17. Kaliro Katono	78
18. Witchcraft in Uganda	81
19. Travelling in East Africa	84
20. Hanging out in East Africa	91
21. Evil spirits in the Village	98
22. Cathie Lee Nursery School	103
23. Jovins	110
24. Teacher Azidah and our loyal staff	112
25. Sisterly Wisdom	121
26. Perfecting the Walk of a Barefoot Priest	123
27. Royalty is my identity, servanthood is my assignment	127
Lessons I've learnt as a woman on mission and in ministry.	135
Treasure Harvest Ministries	138

FOREWORD

For thousands of years, women have played key roles in the New Testament church. Priscilla is one woman that comes to mind (Acts 18:1). Priscilla was involved in sharing her love for God in the marketplace, and assisted in planting churches in Antioch, Ephesus, Corinth and Rome. In the same pioneering spirit, Lesa Tacon has planted a labour of love in the heart of Africa.

Lesa's story contains all the components of a great drama, but it is much, much, more. Set in the mystical continent of Africa, with threats to her life, support from angels, and the kindness of strangers, every chapter is a demonstration of remarkable faith in God. Faith for protection, provision, and divine connections, such as Pastor Robinah.

Lesa's heart of compassion reaches out to people in the most desperate of situations. I've been privileged to have visited her in Uganda, and witnessed this love in action. Walking Africa's dusty village paths, Lesa brings a message of hope to all she meets. Thousands of lives have already been impacted by her selfless nature. One testimony of this is the Cathie Lee Nursery School.

It is my heartfelt prayer, that this book will inspire a new generation of women to arise and share God's heart of love with the world.

Peter Sewell
Hervey Bay, Qld
June 2022

INTRODUCTION

I've always known that I had a calling on my life. When I was growing up, I knew I wanted to be a missionary, not that I really knew what that was, and I wanted to go to Africa.

Later in my life I was told that my Great Aunt, Sister Mary Editha, was a missionary Nun for most of her life in Rabaul, Papua New Guinea.

When my own children were growing up, I used to tell them, 'One day I'm going to live in Africa and you guys can rent my house from me'. We all got used to hearing this so it was no surprise when I finally left for Uganda.

My sister had passed away in 2011 and, still reeling from her early death, I left for Uganda early 2012. I was going to visit the girl I had sponsored for years and to meet her child. This was it! This was my look-see trip. I knew God had called me and I knew there was something for me to do in Africa. I planned a six-week trip to find whatever it was that God was prompting me to do.

After the initial two weeks on an organised insight trip visiting children all over Uganda, I filled the other four weeks volunteering in an orphanage in Kampala and journeying to Gulu in the North of Uganda. Many people's lives there had been devastated by war and many children had been kidnapped and used as child soldiers and sex slaves for years.

Unbeknown to me, eager to do the Lord's work, compassion and passion were to unfold before me, leading to serving God in a unique way, loving and serving the people of Uganda, with many lessons learned along the way. This is my journey.

Lesa Tacon
Hervey Bay, QLD
June 2022

ACKNOWLEDGEMENTS

I would like to acknowledge the different people and teams who have volunteered their time and expertise in coming to Uganda to help build this ministry.

We would not be where we are today without your support and love for us here at Treasure Harvest Ministries. You are valued beyond words and your contribution, small or large, continues to make a difference in many people's lives.

BUILDING TEAM

Troy Sullivan, Michael & Sharaya Crawford, Ashley & Milla Bottrell, Terry & Derylee Bottrell, Adelle Bottrell, Mathew Eden, Steve Forbes, Lester Stratford, Stefan Knoerrlein, Alexander Knoerrlein, Camilla Wehnert, Bernhard Wehnert, Wally Hromis, Rainer Knoerrlein, David Pierson, Luke Strochnetter, Joseph Spannari, Hudson Faulkner and Carlotta Sereni.

CHILDREN'S CAMP AND MINISTRY TEAM

Brenda & Tony Lenthall, Darryl & Judah Greig, Michelle & Daniel Haines, Robyn Vievers, Vickie James and Monika Norris.

MEDICAL CLINICS

Michele Thompson, Dr Vincent Lubangakene, Gail Whitmore and Wendy Gate.

Thank you to everyone that has volunteered their time and expertise in any way.

Lil Star, Peta McNaughton, Peter Sewell, Sue & Tony Thompson, Rosa Czinege, Laura Tschall and the many more I haven't mentioned.

To all of our sponsors, supporters and faithful contributors, you know who you are, we are so thankful and grateful for you. Treasure Harvest Ministries is what it is today because of your sacrifice and love.

I am so thankful for my faithful Ugandan sister Pastor Robinah Kirabo. You are the backbone of this ministry. It truly was a heavenly match putting us together to reach out to those with broken hearts. It is an honour to serve alongside of you. You continue to inspire me with your love, commitment and loyalty to serve people and to see them walk free from constraints and bondages into the arms of our loving saviour Jesus Christ.

For all the precious people in Uganda and beyond, we have been blessed to be a part of your lives and we honour you. It is a privilege to serve you and to help make this life a better one for you. You are the treasure!

Most important of all I give credit to my Lord and Saviour Jesus Christ. I do what I do because of you. With you all things are possible. I love because you first loved me and it is my joy to serve you.

1. CALLING

Finding myself as a single mother to two wonderful children, I became used to making the decisions and doing life on my own from when they were just babies. My children grew and so did my love towards God and people.

I had wonderful opportunities to go on short mission trips into the Pacific Islands and Asia, teaching, loving and serving people wherever I went. My first look at working with people who were HIV+ was in Thailand on a rubbish dump, with a heap of kids, doing a bit of cleaning them up and cutting their nails and loving on them. Then I was part of a team going into the bars of Pattaya and talking with the prostitutes and inviting them to different courses they could access with an organisation to help them out of the dangerous life they were leading. A real eye opener to the realities of life for many.

I had an extremely supportive network of family and friends and a local church all around me. As the kids grew, we were always doing outside activities, camping and bushwalking anything that was healthy and didn't cost a lot to do. I always made the best of every situation even when there were limited funds. I walked by faith not by sight believing in the goodness of God over my life.

My sister came to live in Hervey Bay towards the end of her journey with cancer, when she was forty years old. We had a wonderful two years of fun and laughter and tears before her tragic and untimely death. I suppose this was the catalyst to my wanting to go to Africa and actually putting things in place to go. My children were now grown up and doing their own thing and I felt it was time to fulfil my dream to travel to Africa.

It was incredibly amazing landing in this completely foreign continent that I had dreamed about for so long. I had travelled to poorer countries and spent time with other cultures and felt comfortable around different looking people and poverty.

Uganda is a developing country with over 40 million people living in it. My first impression on landing in Uganda was a complete assault on my senses! There were thousands of people everywhere. Dirt, smoke, cars, motorbikes and people weaving in and out of each other somehow with not too much trouble. I was a part of an organised insight tour so the stress of working everything out for myself on arrival was alleviated somewhat for a couple of weeks. I was feeling quite confident in myself and my abilities to adapt to these new people, circumstances and whole new culture. I had the exciting and long waited for opportunity to connect with a child I had sponsored, who herself was a young mother by then. Years of writing and helping this child and then meeting her as she was finishing the program was so fulfilling in itself. We travelled all over central and southern Uganda experiencing and interacting with the plight and desperation of women and children and seeing how sponsorship was making a difference in their lives. It was a wonderful trip but for me only just touched the surface of what God was doing in my heart. I knew there was much more for me.

Towards the end of the tour, I had noticed the discreet attentions of a local Ugandan man on the trip. I remember feeling completely at a loss of what to do about this but after talking to a trusted friend back in Australia, I felt led to pursue this new interesting emerging relationship.

I continued on with my look-see trip and immersed myself into the work of volunteering my skills in Kampala and north to the town of Gulu I had previously arranged with different organisations. This proved to deepen my love and compassion for the people of Uganda. I went on my first safari to the wonderful Murchison National Park to encounter the African animals and more, and certainly wasn't disappointed. A highlight was seeing the powerful Murchison Falls where the Victoria Nile River surges through a narrow gap over a massive drop into the Nile River. Then it was onward to Rwanda to visit the capital Kigali before I headed back to Australia full of thoughts and ideas about all of my experiences on this amazing journey I was on.

Seven months later I headed back to Uganda for a year to see what was going to eventuate in ministry and my own personal life.

Early days visiting Rwanda and Congo

Early days up country at Katakwi. These boys came out of the bush to greet me

First time in Uganda with my sponsored child and her child

2. CULTURE SHOCK!

Pastor Joel had a school for deaf children in Kampala and was a friend of mine who had visited me in Australia. Joel and his wife had stayed with me for a while and so as I headed back to Uganda, I felt quite sure of my safety as I would be volunteering at his ministry school and would have a base to start my own journey to see where God was leading me.

I stayed in a local guesthouse until I could find a place to rent and went daily to the school in a slum area to learn Ugandan Sign Language and to get to know the children living there so I could help teach them. My days were full of dust and chalk, Posho and Beans, children and love. I would hop on a Boda Boda - motorcycle in the afternoons and go into the city in search of food, a swim in a pool and to explore the bustling city of Kampala. Eventually I moved into a flat in a secure compound not far away from my friends. I had only the bare essentials for living as well as my gear I had brought from Australia. I walked to most places and enjoyed meeting all the locals in the area. Little did I know that I was being watched!

One evening about 8pm as I was finishing eating some fresh fish, I had bought by the side of the road that day, the landlord's young wife appeared at my locked gate and asked me to open. I remember that the other flats were still unoccupied and the landlord was at work so it was just me and the woman and her 3-year-old daughter there at the time. She repeated her request to open the gate but instinct told me to keep it shut. I asked her a number of times if she was ok and because of the language barrier she could only repeat her request to me to please open.

I suppose my compassion and trust made me decide to unlock and open the gate to her as I thought she needed help. Immediately three young African men armed with a panga - machete, a knife and a sharp stabbing iron bar forced their way into the house yelling and pushing the woman and her child in front of them. They were yelling at me and pushed me back into a lounge chair and stood over me with the panga at my throat and the knife at my chest, threatening over and over to kill me. They were demanding all my money and ransacking the house looking for anything of value to them. They took my laptop, phone, tablet and MP3 player and other personal items.

This was all happening quite quickly but to me it seemed surreal and a long time. I was absolutely terrified at one moment and then completely calm and composed in the next. I was praying and asking Jesus what to do and for his help the whole time. One of the men grabbed my purse and dumped the contents out in front of me and picked up some of the cards and a photo of my step grandson. I don't know why but I boldly and calmly snatched the cards, one of which was my ATM card out of his hands and declared, "You don't need them!"

He asked me if the photo was my child. With the panga still at my throat I kept asking Jesus to show me what to do!

I didn't have a clue what to do or how I was going to get out of this alive!

One of the men started to pull me up out of the chair with the intention of dragging me to one of the bedrooms. I'm sure I was going to be locked in it, but I suppose I'll never know. I dropped to the ground and with all my strength and authority that I certainly wasn't feeling, I declared "You are not taking me in there!" I was fighting and holding on to the lounge chair and eventually got back into the chair. Suddenly I threw my arms up into the air, bowed my head down to my lap and shouted, "You're free! You have everything now, you can go, you are free".

One of the men said to me, "You are not going to scream and raise the alarm?" I kept my head down and swore to him that no, I was not going to yell, just go! The next minute everything was silent. I lifted my head and they were gone.

I looked over at the women and her child still huddled on the lounge chair where I had pushed her as I tried to protect them when one of the men tried to approach them. I looked at her and the open door and honestly just couldn't believe that they were gone, and that I was unhurt! I got up and paced the floor and tried to shut the door but realised they had taken the keys so it couldn't be locked. Out of the corner of my eye I noticed the woman bring a small mobile phone out of wherever she had been hiding it. This was incredible to me and I asked her why did she still have her mobile phone! Why didn't they take it? Did she have credit on it? She offered it to me and I searched around on the floor for any papers with the phone numbers of anyone I knew on them, who could come to my aid. Thankfully I found phone numbers for two people that I knew could be trusted and could help me and called them for help.

A LIFE WORTH LIVING

What seemed like hours later, but was actually soon after the attack and robbery, there was a knock on the outside compound steel gate and someone called out, identifying himself as police. I was in shock and disbelief at what had just happened and so I refused to come out of the house to open the gate. I was trusting no one! I don't know how they eventually gained access but suddenly the compound was full of police. It really was just a blur for me as I was in shock and disbelief. Two friends of mine turned up in their vehicles. While trying to comfort me, knowing that this had been an extremely dangerous and traumatic experience for me, they helped pack up all my belongings as I tried to engage with the police about what had happened. They then transported me and my small amount of gear I still had to a safer house for that night.

I suppose this incident was the catalyst for a number of events that were about to take place. There were some very important life decisions I had to make. I went down to the local police station the next morning to make a statement and was informed that they were taking the landlord's wife into custody as she was suspected of being involved with the robbery. I was really shaken up about this but this was something I didn't want to happen to this young mum. The holding cell was visible to me, full of women tightly squeezed into a small round room peering out of small barred holes in the wall. An agreement was made that I would be paid back the three months' rent I had paid in advance and the police would do what they could to track down the men who had stolen my items and committed this crime.

The investigation went on for a long time with no leads or advances and to this day I have four or five robbery investigations going on in Kampala! At the time I almost took out the award for the most robbed Mzungu in Uganda!

3. TAKING BACK GROUND AND OPPORTUNITIES ARISE

The hunt was on for accommodation. I had decided to continue on with my mission in Uganda and to take back the ground that the enemy had stolen from me! There was no turning back, only onwards and upwards for me, as I would often say to myself.

A friend of mine helped me to find a suitable flat in a secure compound on the other side of Kampala. I threw myself into the life and culture of Uganda. I continued to ride on the back of a Boda Boda, motorcycle, over to the Deaf School. I also came across another position as a volunteer teacher, teaching English to a group of women living with HIV. I was tutoring children in a primary school with reading and writing support, teaching creative writing and general support in all classes. As if that wasn't enough, I was also involved with an active ministry combating child sacrifice in Uganda and beyond.

I rode an hour out of Kampala to a village every week to teach women English. I would walk through this village visiting different people and would often stop at an old lady's home. She was blind and made her living by making baskets out of papyrus and banana fibre. I would always buy one of her baskets to support her and take time to talk with her. She lived in such poor conditions with a dirt floor and a small bed in her house. She just sat on the floor making her baskets and was content with the life she had. It was easy to make friends with these gentle and happy people regardless of the conditions they lived in.

Around this time some fellow missionaries from Australia, whom I had met previously in Uganda, moved to Uganda and moved in with me. This seemed to be a good idea as safety was the concern for us all at this time.

We were about to be robbed again!

About 3 o'clock in the morning something woke me. Immediately I realised the door to my room was wide open, not as I'd left it when I went to sleep. I reached for my bag already knowing it was gone! Five of us were sleeping in the house that night, four Mzungus and a young lady from the Karamajong from Northern Uganda. I jumped up raising the alarm and switching on lights calling out that the doors were all open. Everyone started to wake responding with cries of 'It's gone!' 'My phone, my laptop they're gone!'

We were on the second floor of a three-story building and as I ran to the open balcony doors, I realised I must have scared off the robbers when I started calling out as they had left a huge computer screen sitting on the balcony, ready to be lowered down to the waiting thief's arms.

The landlord had been alerted and had called the police who had come outfitted with German Shepherd dogs and there seemed to be a bit of a chase on as we had seen the thieves running away. Nothing was found that early morning, so it was down to the police station when it was light to file yet another report. Strangely days later my bag was found and handed in to the police with the contents and my ATM card but the money in the bag was gone. I was beginning to realise that I definitely was a target as a white person in this beautiful but dangerous land.

On another occasion I was travelling from church to a friend's home to pray for her sick little boy. I jumped on a Matatu on a main road and missed the fact that it had only male occupants. They seemed to be courteous and happy and insisted that I have a seat in the front where the seatbelt was. We travelled on and they were quite jovial and seemed to really want to take care of me. Unfortunately, unbeknown to me, they were stealing my purse, phone and whatever was of value in my bag. They were so sneaky and good at it, I had no idea! Eventually the Matatu pulled over and they made an excuse that I had to get out and get into the back. As I was getting out I had my two bags pushed at me. One of the men slammed the door and with a look of steel in his eyes that I will never forget, coldly said to me, "you get another taxi!"

I knew in my heart right then that I had been robbed. I searched my bag and sure enough my purse and phone were gone. I had no idea where I was and burst into tears of shock. I stumbled down the dirt road to a roadside shop belonging to a Muslim man. He was gracious enough to see I was upset and in shock so immediately brought a chair for me to sit on as he tried to calm me. I felt that I could request his help as I searched my bag for any paper that had a phone number of someone who could come and help me. Finally, I found the only number I had, that of a lady Pastor that I had also travelled to Jinja with for a few days before this incident and gotten to know.

The Muslim shopkeeper called her and told her what had happened and where I was. This dear lady immediately got on a Boda Boda and came to where I was. What a relief it was to see a familiar face and to know that she could take charge now and help me out of this awful situation. I can't express how much I felt alone and helpless. To see someone you trust makes the difference between despair and confidence. She took me to the nearest police station where again I gave my story and statement in the hope of tracking these harmful people down and bringing justice to my situation.

I was told how lucky I was as this was happening to others frequently and some people were hurt and even killed for their belongings by these thugs masquerading as taxi drivers.

Early days in a remote village.
I would buy these baskets from this lady to help support her.

4. SURVIVAL OF THE FITTEST

In Uganda there seems to be so much corruption. In a land of tremendous beauty and gentle hearted people with smiles and laughter in their faces, in the midst of unimaginable suffering there are those who are out to steal, kill and destroy from all around them. Life can be unfair and beautiful, kind people suffer. It is such a different culture and life from the one I had grown up in. Everything was different. Not necessarily wrong but just different.

I suppose that is how I survived my first couple of years living in the African culture after the initial excitement and adventure had worn off. I would remind myself of this phrase often. I would think to myself, God you have put me in the slowest place on earth. Nothing would happen when you wanted it to. It would take place days even weeks later! I was used to the fast pace of life living in a western country and culture where things could be arranged and happen virtually straight away.

Africans are an event-oriented people not time-oriented like people from a country like Australia. This means that an event like a ceremony is planned and because families are large and dispersed, they will have to travel from all over to get to the ceremony. This could take days so therefore the ceremony will go for a long period of time, sometimes days, as people keep arriving. They will be looked after, given accommodation and meals until it is over.

I was immersed in a population of 40+ million and living in the capital city of Kampala with over 2 million other people. There were traffic and people jams everywhere. The streets were alive with people at midnight! You could get almost anything you wanted anytime day or night if it could be produced.

Ugandans are a very entrepreneurial people. There are pop up shops all over the sides of every road and lane in Kampala, selling fruit and vegetables, shoes, clothes, mobile phone accessories, furniture and many other items necessary or not for daily living. If you see a young man walking along with a bucket on his head full of nail grooming items, and a small stool, it is his business. You can stop walking, sit down and get your toenails and fingernails cleaned, manicured and polished to a 5-star level for a very small charge.

There are Saloons [hair salons] everywhere up and down the roads. They are constantly being used by men, women and children for haircuts, shaves for school children and planting hair pieces. This is big business in Uganda.

The women are embarrassed if they haven't got the hair styles called weaves, woven into their short curly hair. They want longer styles like other women from cultures where hair grows long and straight or wavy. It takes lots of maintenance to get their own hair to grow and then they straighten it with chemicals, which can be costly for them. The weave can create the style they want and be left in for months. I would wonder why I saw so many women patting their heads all the time. This was a polite way to stop the itch! It is also government regulation for school children in Uganda to shave their heads for uniformity and neatness.

5. HEALING BROKEN HEARTS

I was teaching English once a week to women living with HIV after a midweek church service that they attended. I remember arriving for my lesson early and joining in with the service. This was my introduction to my wonderful sister and friend, Pastor Robinah.

When I entered the service, I felt the awesome presence of God and was quite captured with the presence of the Pastor sharing at the front of the room. I slipped into the back and tried to blend in. After the service I taught the group of women English for a couple of hours. We had a great time together learning and playing some games. I always try to make it as interesting, varied and fun when teaching English lessons to any age. The next week after my lesson the lady Pastor approached me and humbly introduced herself to me. She asked if I would come with her to pray for a woman suffering from Sickle Cell Anaemia. When I had finished praying for the lady, I thought, wow, that was a powerful prayer prayed with such authority like I had not prayed before. Over the next weeks Robinah and I developed a friendship.

I was invited to a Ugandan wedding and I went with Robinah as it was a mutual friend getting married. I had begun to feel very comfortable around her and it was great

A LIFE WORTH LIVING

to be able to attend with her. What a colourful and joyous and flamboyant wedding it was! People were plentiful, as was the food. The bride changed outfits at least four times as did the bridesmaids and the whole event went all day, well into the night with lots of music and speeches. Emphasis was on the different families there and individual wedding cakes were given to them. It was a huge affair and as in most ceremonies, everyone contributes with money or donates food. I needed to leave early before it got too late at night as it could be dangerous riding around on a Boda Boda in the dark, especially for a white person and a woman.

Robinah was also ready to leave so I asked her if it would be ok for me to visit her home and children on the way as she didn't live too far away. We walked through the slums and finally came to her home. It was a simple cement block house in an open compound with three small rooms. The middle room had a couch and an old TV in it and was called the sitting room. Either side was a bedroom, one with three bunks a small single bed and a kitchen of sorts consisting of a small charcoal stove, pots, plates and utensils. This is where the food was prepared and cooked. The other room had a double bed in it. The toilet/latrine and bathing room were outside and were used by all the families living in the compound. I visited briefly and met her three delightful children and then it was time for me to head home.

Robinah and I started to meet together for a coffee and a swimming lesson once a week as I was also teaching a couple of Ugandan ladies I had met to swim. These were fun times keeping these ladies afloat while friendships were growing.

As the friendship deepened between Robinah and I, we realised that we were pursuing the same passion to serve God and to minister to women with broken hearts.

Around this time my own heart was also breaking. The man I had met a year beforehand and thought that he might actually be the one for me, was betraying me in a terrible way. God was working in me helping me through this time. It was ironic, I was asking God to show me this man's heart towards me and He was teaching me a lot about my own heart and the need to guard it fiercely. Thank goodness for Robinah's help and guidance through this traumatic time. Her trusted friendship and insights into the culture and this situation were so valuable to me as I didn't have the same cultural understandings at this time.

We had arranged to meet, the three of us to sort out things but he didn't turn up. Another time I received a very disturbing phone call from him accusing me of going to his home and setting people on him to kill him! I really understood then that I was in a dangerous and volatile situation that I needed to get out of.

He had actually taken me to meet his family in Soroti. He was a very dark and tall Iteso man with an air of authority and leadership. He had told me he was a Christian, and he portrayed attributes of a godly man in every way, so I had no reason to doubt this. As they say, love can make you blind, and I saw only what I wanted to see. Thank God for Robinah who caught on to what was really happening and spoke truth into the matter or sadly there could have been a very different outcome for me.

Robinah and I continued to pray into our vision and to brainstorm ways we could actually start a ministry that we both felt called to in Africa.

Lesa and Robinah in traditional clothes

6. DESTINY

I returned to Australia to work and put things in order so I could return to Uganda fresh. I was ready to pursue setting up and starting a ministry to broken hearted women and their children who were living in poor and desperate situations in the slums of Kampala.

Robinah had been able to locate a house in the slums of a poor area in Kampala. Kawempe division was highly populated by Muslims and it was also the area where I had been attacked and robbed a year before. I was headed back to the danger zone but I trusted God and that He had a plan. Shortly after arriving back in Uganda we had a short trip to Tanzania and over to the Island of Zanzibar.

Tanzania was completely different to Uganda having a higher Muslim population with Arabic influences, with the huge city capital, Dar Es Salaam.

Robinah was a hit with the locals. She was wearing her hair in dreadlocks and the people on the island loved her. I felt completely at ease and safe with her. This was a first for her. First time in a plane, first time to see the ocean and to swim in it.

Robinah has a commanding presence about her. She can be serious but also playful and joyous. She has a deep sense of peace and is highly respected and sought after by people of all ages. A mother, a Pastor, evangelist, teacher, leader and counsellor to many. I was so happy to be able to be a part of her opportunity to experience other places and cultures. We had a fantastic time on Zanzibar learning from the people and sharing the love of Christ with them.

Wherever we went we ministered for Jesus. That's who I am. I am a minister of reconciliation between man and God. I am a laid down lover of Jesus Christ and I live my life for Him. As I have become more assured of who I am in Him, I have learnt to walk out that victorious living each day in my life. I don't worry about my future because it is secure in Him. I have truly learnt to walk by faith not by sight. I also am sure that, what doesn't kill me only makes me stronger. Stronger in Christ!

In the slums of Kampala with children in my neighbourhood

7. BEGINNINGS

Back in Kampala, ministry had begun. We had walked through our neighbourhood up and down the dirty, dusty and at times muddy paths of the slum. We stopped to greet and meet people. We talked with different women about their lives and invited them to a meeting to be held at our house to talk about the skill building classes we were going to start, and to find out the interest in these.

At our very first meeting fifteen women showed up. This was exciting and showed that there was definite interest. They were happy that something good and useful had come to their neighbourhood. We decided that we would hold daily classes teaching English, Paper bead, Jewellery design and Sewing/Tailoring.

There was a mixture of Muslim and Christian older and younger ladies, some with babies and young children. Classes were Monday to Friday starting with a devotional time and finishing around 1pm which also happened to be the Muslim call to prayer time, so it was almost like a bell to let everyone know we were finishing, very convenient for us. In the afternoons at 4pm we opened again for drumming and cultural dance practice. We had found a young Muslim couple who were dance and drum instructors and they were willing to come three days a week to teach our ladies. This was a wonderful opportunity for the women and brought a lot of fun and laughter to the ministry. This young couple eventually gave their lives to Jesus as they heard and saw the love of Jesus in action. They eventually had a baby girl whom I had the honour of naming Glorious Destiny, Gloria for short.

We were able to help start our very own traditional dance group which went on to perform all over the country at different functions. They were available for all our ceremonies and parties we have held over the years. One year some of the members even went to Japan to perform.

About this time Shamira brought her younger sister Elena to meet us. She had been rescued from a village life of torture and abuse and brought to Kampala to live with them in their one room block house. Elena was about 11 years old, had never been to school and had spent her young life working as a slave for the people she lived with, cooking, cleaning and digging in the garden. She was a very traumatised girl as she had been made to eat human flesh from fresh corpses.

In Uganda there is a phenomenon known as a 'Nightdancer'. There is witchcraft involved. It is supposedly someone who runs through a village at night looking for fresh dead bodies in graves. When found, they use witchcraft to exhume the body and take it home, cut up the flesh and feed this to their family. This is a well-known and feared practice often reported in the media. Incidences of child sacrifice also happen in communities where children are taken and body parts removed, leaving the child either dead or maimed for life! The body parts are used for ceremonial uses by witchdoctors for power and wealth. I have seen and worked with villages and children who have survived this terrible abuse, left without certain body parts, hacked into and left as disabled and disfigured children. I have been involved with an organisation and individuals who live to combat and end child sacrifice in Uganda.

When we started working with Elena, she was quite erratic in her behaviour. If she was left alone she would cut up and destroy her clothes and bedding where she lived. She would eat all the food that had been cooked for the family meal for that day if it was left unattended. I started to teach her some basic English and to build a trust relationship between us.

Elena showed us her stomach. There were small cuts and scars all over her from where she had been drained of her blood to be used by her abusers for evil intent. We were able to locate a local school willing to work with her and enrolled her in the first year. We gave her her first uniform, which brought her a sense of belonging and boosted her confidence. Elena seemed to thrive at school but unfortunately her behaviour was still erratic at home. When her sister had a baby, they had no choice but to send her to an Aunt in another village. The young couple just couldn't cope with her anymore and even though we tried to help in different ways, she was sent away. This is a sad fact of ministry that sometimes things don't work out the way you would hope for, but you just have to trust God and His bigger plan.

In Uganda it is about survival of the fittest! There is a culture of polygamy where a man can take more than one wife and have children continuously one after another, then can discard a former wife and take another. This can be a very hard life for the women and children. Life expectancy is an average of 52 years and half the population is under 14 years old. A lot of women were coming to our classes with the saddest stories of neglect and abuse and most of them were HIV+. The need was immense and we were doing what we could, loving and supporting these families by buying food, sacks of maize flour called Posho. We bought beans and rice to distribute to the ones with nothing to eat, provided school fees to some of their children and housed the ones with nowhere to live. We were counselling the women who were HIV+ and paying their transport to get to the hospital to get their medication. We would provide extra nutritious food for these women as their normal diet of posho and beans was not sufficient in the nutrients they needed to survive.

One of the ladies that had come to us at the beginning of our ministry was clearly wasting away from this disease. Topista was a single mum of three boys, one of whom was living with her. The oldest was living in the village with family members and the youngest had been taken to the Democratic Republic of Congo by a family. Topista had moved to Kampala to access medical support for HIV after losing her husband. She needed her son Allan, who was only 11 years old, to care for her when she was unable to care for herself.

HIV Aids is stigmatized throughout Uganda and if you are positively diagnosed, especially if you live in a village, people feel fear of being discriminated against and not being accepted by others. This leaves them with the physical and emotional challenges from being unaccepted and outcast by everyone around them.

When Topista found her way to us it was important that she felt loved and accepted by us straight away. We found and acquired accommodation for her and her son, set up a food program for them and enrolled Allan in a day school. With support we were able to set Topista up with a small income generating business - Mushroom Farming. We helped her get started by sourcing the right training for her, getting the equipment and building the structure the mushrooms would grow in. Then we taught her how to build a market to sell the produce. We made sure she was getting the right nutritious food to help with the anti-retroviral drugs she was taking and paid for her transport to the hospital weekly.

Topista thrived and eventually after a couple of years was well enough to find work with a Pastor in a local church. She continued to get well with no sign of sickness and I believe she has been totally healed. Topista continues to visit our ministry and joins us faithfully whenever we do evangelistic ministry in the community.

Ladies enjoying a game of volleyball after class in Kampala

Sharing a meal together in the early days in Kampala

Beading class in the early days in Kampala

8. SMALL FIRE – LARGE FLAME

I continued to move in and out of Africa, coming home for a break to see my family and to raise awareness and needed funds to further the work. Eventually we knew that God was extending the ministry to make further impact beyond Kampala and out into a village where the people have little opportunities, unlike in the city. We started to look for land in villages outside Kampala in all directions. We would travel with different agents or Brokers as they were called into the countryside once or twice a week to look at land. We would pray and ask God if this was where He wanted ministry to continue. I had raised enough funds through generous people in Australia to purchase some acres. I had a big vision!

My vision was to love people and to reach out to the poor and needy, the hurting and lost. Treasure Harvest Ministries brings healing for broken hearts, speaks up for those who cannot speak for themselves, stands with and empowers people, especially woman and children, so they can make their own decisions and live a better, more purposeful life.

I truly believe that God has a plan and a purpose for our lives, a good plan for every single one of us! We are all uniquely made with talents, gifts and abilities that belong to us. Sometimes we just need to reach out and stand beside someone to help them see that in themselves. Maybe even walk part of their journey with them. There is nothing to prove. We all bring something to the table. Nobody is a mistake and every life matters.

One day we travelled with a couple of brokers out to the town of Wobelenzi and out along a dirt road through a small trading centre to a place called Kaliro Katono, which means small fire! We were shown two acres of bush land, cultivated with Coffee, Cassava, Mango and Jackfruit trees. We knew straight away that this was where we were to buy. We walked around and met the neighbours who were very poor families, lots of children living basic lives in the dirt. The local chairman of the village also lived close by, which could be handy.

Negotiations began with the owner of the land, an elderly Muslim man. We brought out a surveyor and engaged the services of a lawyer. After quite a few meetings with the entire family of the owner about ten people, we settled on the price and had a ceremony at the land where the legal Land Title and land became ours. The old man inked his thumb followed by other family members and made his print on the documents. The document for the Land Title still had to come through so we had to wait for it.

I had spoken to other people, especially whites, about owning land and titles in Uganda. It was well known that people were still waiting years after purchasing land for the Title to come through. Unbelievably we had the Land Title within two months after purchase. This was great confirmation that we had been brought to the right place at the right time and met the right people. We were on the right track!

First thing I did was fence the land with trees cut from the land and barbed wire. We had big plans! The first thing that was needed was a habitable dwelling and so the ministry house began. I arrived at the block with the builder and his first question to me was, 'What do you want built?' I really didn't have a clue what I was doing but I'd done a bit of research on good old Google and had a bit of an idea what to build so I said "Just make it square sir!"

We walked out the size that I wanted, which consisted of two main bedrooms with bathrooms in them and a front area for kitchen and dining. Simple, comfortable does the job with a veranda part way around. It had to have large windows and doors so plenty of light could get in. This was so different to the houses the village people build with such tiny windows so no light can get in. They build this way because of lack of money and safety as they usually can't afford the cost of a larger window with security bars and glass.

Over the next year, as God provided, the ministry house continued to be built and finished little by little. Eventually we were able to bring electricity into the land which is a miraculous story in itself.

Pastor Robinah was negotiating and organising with the electrical supply company to bring in a couple of poles off the dirt main road and supply to our little bush home. It's unheard of to get jobs like this one done in under six months, with lots of negotiating. Unbeknown to us the whole village of Kaliro Katono had their supply cut months before as someone had literally cut the wires, and they had no sense of reconnection happening anytime soon. When Robinah heard of their predicament she did what she always does and that is to pray. Within two days of speaking to the authorities the power was reconnected and back on in the village.

Robinah drove out from Kampala for a midweek Bible study meeting at our place and was greeted by loud adulation from the African women. Not understanding what was happening, she asked someone what was happening.

"It's for you Pastor, you have brought us back the electricity! We know that there are two directors, you and your sister, the white director and the black director."

I have been lovingly known as and called The White Director, Teacher Lesa, Auntie Lesa, Jjaja, Mummy and the Mother of the church, in Uganda. When I first started going to Uganda, I was given the name Mukisa, which means blessing, by a Pastor in a church that I was fellowshipping at. Those days I travelled by Boda Boda everywhere. Sometimes I'd have to catch a Matatu taxi, although I didn't like getting in as they were always overcrowded. I had to push my way in, usually cutting myself on a sharp metal bit protruding from somewhere only to be squashed in between others, smelling the breathtaking aromas of all the people in the taxi!

Twice I was asked if I could change a fifty thousand shilling note for something smaller. Thinking I could help out I did so only to be given a counterfeit note. The second time this occurred I was with Robinah in a Matatu. As we were leaving the taxi, I became aware of it and got really angry, so I enlisted the help of a passing Boda, jumped on and chased the taxi! Unfortunately, it got away in all the traffic.

We pulled over where there were Traffic Police to make a complaint. Although being very sorry for my loss, they were unable to catch the culprits. This is a big issue in Uganda and is just added to the corruption and people with intentions which are not good in their hearts.

9. DIVINE CONNECTIONS

Eventually we planted Harvest Church under a Mango tree on our land. Lots of people, especially children and young adults, started attending weekly.

We needed to construct some sort of rudimentary structure for shelter before the wet season when everything turns to slippery, wet mud.

About this time, we had a visitor from Australia who was a nurse who came to run a medical clinic for us. One year I was traveling to Uganda through Johannesburg Airport and on the final stretch into Entebbe when I happened to meet another Australian woman also traveling to Uganda. This was what I call a divine meeting. She was on her way up to Irene Gleeson Foundation in Kitgum, Northern Uganda. We had an hour conversation which led to connecting and following each other's lives and work for a couple of years. This led to her coming to our ministry to run a medical clinic in our village.

Michele sourced and teamed up with a wonderful young Ugandan Doctor and together we ran a three-day medical clinic in the village where more than two hundred women, men and children were seen and received quality medical assistance and help for the many different ailments diagnosed.

It was an incredible outcome to a divine encounter between two Aussie women two years before.

A funny thing happened to me while we conducted the clinic. As the rain came down, making the land a very muddy and slippery place, I was on my way to the pit latrine and slipped over in front of all the patients and actually broke my finger. I was picked up with mud splattered all over me, laughing and crying in pain at the same time. The ladies washed me off and after the shock I went back to my job as the pharmacy dispenser and nurse, distributing the medication as prescribed by the doctor. No time for a broken finger! Thankfully it healed well in the next few weeks.

One of the common complaints we kept hearing throughout the clinic was, "I have syphilis!" After a while we realised that there had been a lot of misinformation and misdiagnoses by local clinicians. It was more likely to be a Urinary Tract Infection or Thrush. There were also a lot of eye conditions especially amongst the elderly, which probably had its roots in poor dietary nutrition. Although a lot of different nutritious foods are grown in Uganda, a lot of people seem to eat only the starchy foods that fill them and not enough fruit and vegetables high in vitamins and minerals. Unless you grow it, it will cost money, so with the little they have people are forced to buy food like Posho, rice and beans that fill the bellies of families with many kids. So they miss out on the nutrients from a variety of foods.

I put Vitamin A drops in many eyes over the clinic days. A lot of children presented with Malaria which we were able to treat. It was a really valuable and fun event and much needed in the community. We have held medical outreach clinics numerous times since this first one, even going into remote villages. One clinic was held over three days with a team from Australia and our Ugandan Doctor. During this clinic there was a freak storm through the village. We sheltered in a small room that we were using as the base and I remember thinking this could be the end as it was so severe. When it was over we had a lot of hurt people to patch up. Overall we saw and helped close to 1000 people at this clinic.

Another time an Australian friend came to spread some of his expertise, love and smiles our way. We had an awesome time of Business Training at our two bases in Kampala and in the village. Both were well attended, informative and fun. Everyone attending went away with a lot more knowledge and insight to put into practice.

Harvest Church, planted in May 2017 was increasing in number. Each week more people would arrive so we had to build a structure to keep the rain and sun off the people. We used local labourers for most of the construction. Up went rough wooden poles and iron sheets with windows cut in them. Plastic sheeting, papyrus and any fibrous material was used until we had a rudimentary structure with a dirt floor that we filled up with crude wooden benches. We had a usable structure that was totally packed out every Sunday, so much so that within a year it had to be broken apart to be made bigger.

Lots of teaching and discipleship was happening in this place with different groups for the different talents and gifts that were emerging. Prayer, Bible Study, Youth, Children, Singing and Music, Evangelism, English lessons, Sewing and Beading were some. Crusades and Conferences were also arranged. Outreach into the community was going well.

I remember my first Crusade I was a part of in the bush in rural Uganda. The locals knocked together a simple wooden raised structure with a platform for the speakers and singers to perform and preach from. I've seen men hitting them together with hammers even when the people are crowded on them, Ha! The sound system and large speakers are brought in and turned up and up! There is only one volume and that is loud. The people start to arrive late afternoon and into the evening. Children and women gather first then as the darkness of night comes and everything gets hyped and louder, the men filter in. The preaching is powerful and many hearts are moved and repentance is present. Usually a film is shown and is very well attended as most village people don't have TV. Sometimes the power is cut off or more often the generator runs out of fuel, as has happened at most of the crusades I've attended. Most people respond positively at these events and have a true heart response to the Gospel.

I've climbed up onto these very rickety platforms, been handed a microphone and preached a simple message of God's love and many people have come forward for prayer. I've clambered down again, not very gracefully and prayed for a lot of people to receive freedom, healing and deliverance in their lives. At times late into the night.

That is one thing I do a lot of in Africa, also in Australia. There is always someone to pray for or with. I have seen and experienced wonderful answers to prayer over the years and God's awesome provision over individuals, myself and Treasure Harvest Ministries.

On a number of occasions, we have had young women come to us requesting Robinah and I to pray for them to be able to conceive a child. The couples had been trying to fall pregnant for years with no success, so we have agreed together for a miracle. Each time the women have come back nine to twelve months later with a beautiful bundle of joy!

A LIFE WORTH LIVING

I've had the privilege of naming quite a number of babies in Uganda. One time I was teaching at a local school and my fellow teacher went into labour. I went straight from class to the local clinic where she had walked to to give birth and stayed with her while she was in labour, rubbing her back and encouraging her. When it started to get late, I knew I needed to make my way home otherwise it would be too dangerous to go. I'd only just left when she gave birth to a beautiful baby boy whom they named Favour.

Another time we had to take Martha to the clinic in labour. We stayed with her as it was her first baby and she was having a hard time coping with the contractions and the pain. I managed to coax her into walking around the clinic grounds to help with the pain and getting ready for the delivery. Baby Blessing was born that evening but Mum and because of his small size and being premature, had to be transferred to Malago Hospital, the large public hospital in Kampala. Blessing continues to grow into a dear little boy but battles with chesty coughs and breathing issues.

Another time Robinah's cousin had given birth in the hospital and we went to visit. Immediately the mother placed this baby boy in my arms and asked me to name him. As I held him, I asked the Holy Spirit to give me a name for him. Immediately I thought of Joshua from the Bible, which means Jehovah is generous or Jehovah saves, and so he was named Joshua.

What a privilege and an absolute honour to be asked to name these beautiful babies and to watch them grow into their destinies.

Pastor Robinah under the mango tree where we planted Harvest Church

We just bought our land in the village and it needs to be cleared

Dr Vincent writes a script for one of the many patients at a medical clinic held on site

Triage at a remote medical clinic

Our first church building

Inside the first church building

Remote village medical clinic

Preaching a message in church with Pastor Robinah interpreting

Lesa cooking Posho and Beans for workers in our old village style kitchen

10. BEAUTIFUL WOMEN

I find the Ugandan culture to be one of respect, especially concerning older people. Children are taught and required to kneel when greeting any person older than themselves. This doesn't stop as they grow older as adult women kneel in greeting all of their life.

Ugandan people take a lot of pride in their appearance, hoping to look 'smart' as they wash and polish their shoes, suits and shirts - and my favourite, the ladies wearing their high heeled shoes in the dirt and mud through the slums! It means so much to these women, rich or poor, to have their hair done with the latest weave-in style. This is planted or tied into their own hair and kept on for as long as possible. It is quite amusing for westerners to see them patting their heads over and over from what must be an itchy scalp or maybe whatever it is crawling around under the wig! When it rains the women cover their heads with a black plastic bag to keep the rain off the weave as they go about their daily chores of digging, shopping, and selling at the local small business enterprises they have set up.

They are also great entrepreneurs and we try to help where possible, setting the women up in their own small businesses.

One of our ladies, Topista, started her own Mushroom Growing business with our help. We helped her rent some land from a local Pastor and with the funds from the paper bead necklaces that the ladies had made and sold, they bought some pigs to start Pig Farming. We worked together to demolish an old wooden structure on the side of the road where we lived, bought the old wood and transported it to the land we had rented. We built a piggery to house the pigs and the ladies took turns to feed, water and look after them as they grew to a size where they could be sold for a profit.

At the same time Topista's Oyster Mushrooms were sprouting in another small building on the land. We watched over her as she used a 44-gallon drum to cook and prepare the seeds for planting in plastic bags, then hung to grow and finally harvested for sale in the community.

Meanwhile the pigs weren't doing so well as they were getting sick. Even though they tried to get the right help for them, unfortunately they all died. This was a learning experience for us all. The ladies decided to use the profits from the beads the next time for something different, eventually dividing them up amongst themselves for school fees for their kids. We ended up moving the Mushroom Project to our place and more women got involved. It was quite successful until a disease attacked and the crop was lost.

Not to worry, 'Shoes' were the next income generating project! These ladies may have been knocked down but they certainly knew how to get back up again and again!

We had so many different women coming to the ministry with diverse issues. Looking after and educating children was a big one.

Babirye was a young girl about sixteen years old, the oldest child in a large single parent family. Her mother lived in one

A LIFE WORTH LIVING

room with many small children and worked at a local school as the cook. She just didn't have enough money to continue Babirye's education, as happens a lot in Uganda, as the other children also needed some sort of start to their education. The children rarely complete primary or secondary education due to lack of money for fees. The parents themselves have rarely completed their own education so they don't place value on educating their child, sometimes even prioritising child labour over education.

Babirye's mother made the decision to send her to her paternal grandmother's house to live with her and that's how we met her. The grandmother had heard about our classes and sent her to learn some skills in the hope of employment in her future. Her father was not supporting her at all.

The culture of polygamy is such that a man can just walk out on his wife and children and take another wife and start having more children with her. The first wife is left to take care of the children, trying to find enough work just to feed them, often with no help from the father. School fees are another issue and a huge pressure for them.

Babirye started coming to our different lessons and eventually shared her story with us. We were able to meet with her mother and grandmother, and her father, and help get her back to school.

The alternative can be devastating for these young girls. Early marriage or pregnancy or the risk of HIV can continue the cycle of poverty in their lives. Babirye was able to complete two more years of schooling with our help. Unfortunately, she made some bad decisions and chose a wrong path but hopefully her extended family were able to keep supporting her. Not every story has a happy ending.

Martha was twenty-four years old when we met her. She was from the Basoga Tribe from the district of Jinja. Martha like so many others, was born to a young girl. When she was five, she was taken to her fathers' village to live with her Gran. She was not allowed to go to school but sent to dig in the garden and treated like a slave. The police intervened when she was seven and made her Gran enrol her in school. After three weeks she was pulled out and made to hide in the bush and continue to dig. Her Gran lied to the Local Chairman of the village, telling him she was in school, until she was fifteen years old! In all that time she was treated very badly and with cruelty.

One year an Aunt came to the village to give birth and noticed that Martha was only given food every second day, her wild ways and how cruelly she was being treated. When she protested for Martha, the Gran told the Aunt to take her. The Aunt left without her but not before informing the police who took the Gran to prison and located her mother. The Aunt came back for Martha and took her to Kampala to work as a domestic housemaid for four dollars a month. Martha never received any of that money and was moved from place to place until she was eighteen. Martha met her husband when she was eighteen, a well-educated and working man who literally saved her from the circumstances that she was in. Because she had not been schooled and she couldn't speak English, this was a huge barrier to her which left her quite sad as she desired to move forward in her life. One day she met a lady called Victor in the marketplace who told her about a ministry teaching English for free. Martha came along to Treasure Harvest Ministries and her whole life changed. She learnt to write her name for the first time in her life and she was totally involved with all the skilling classes offered.

A LIFE WORTH LIVING

Martha desired one thing above all else and that was to have a child. They had been trying for a long time and had not been able to conceive. Martha learnt about God and His incredible love for her through our love for her and the devotions we held every day before class. She made a decision to place her life into His hands, surrendering her life to Jesus Christ. She asked us to pray for her to conceive a child and brought her husband to meet us. He was so thankful for what we were doing in Martha's life and also made the same decision in his life. Within twelve months Martha and her husband became the happy parents of a beautiful little boy named Blessing.

Another beautiful soul I've had the privilege of getting to know over the years in Uganda is a lady called Sauda. She was somewhere in her forties when I met her. A small, thin lady unfortunately with very few teeth left in her mouth. She was married to a Muslim man with five children and was also a grandmother. She worked very hard to make ends meet, rising early to walk to a local food market to buy the cheaper produce maize so she could cook it and sell it in the evenings.

I would come across her in the evenings as I took my evening walk in the slums, with a large tin saucepan carried on her head, full of steaming hot cobs of maize for sale. She would spend hours walking through the trading centre offering the food snack to people coming home from their work. This was one of her industrious ways of generating a small income for her family. She also washed clothes and any other job she could find so her family could survive.

Sauda found her way to Treasure Ministries very early on when we started and as much as she could she would turn up for classes. She loved the Devotion time we set aside before each class started for the day, to learn about God's love for us, and she participated enthusiastically.

One day Sauda made a choice and surrendered her life to Jesus, committing to follow Him and to make Him her Lord and saviour. This caused a problem for her life as the man she lived with was a Muslim. She continued to live with him and faithfully love him but as time went on and she grew in her faith, her husband grew resentful and threw her out with some of the children. We were able to help Sauda in this crisis with accommodation and help set her up with a small charcoal business. We also helped one of her daughter's continue at school. Unfortunately, Sauda's husband grew bitter at Sauda as she was making her own choices in her life. Her husband barged his way into the ministry one day disrupting classes with the intent to harm Robinah. Fortunately, all the ladies there at the time for a sewing class were able to come to Robinah's aid and the man was arrested by police. The police locked him away in a cell and left him there. Robinah tried to intervene for him even calling his local Muslim elder to talk to him but he refused to admit to his breaking the law and held fast to what he saw as his right to use violence in the situation.

When I returned to Uganda weeks later, he was still in prison and there had been no progress on his case. I was concerned and so asked Robinah to follow up on what was happening. To our horror we found him very sick and dying in the jail. He was ready to comply with police and the law of not taking matters into his own hands. We had no choice but to ask for his release as he was really unwell and could die in the jail if he was left there.

Months went by quietly and then one day he ambushed his sixteen-year-old daughter and tried to drag her off to be married to a much older man. Again, our ladies heard the girl screaming, just outside our gate, and came to her rescue pulling her away from him. This man had done a lot to hurt his family even bursting into the school where his daughter was studying and demanding she leave because it wasn't a Muslim school! These are just some of the problems and issues that evolve in people's lives in Uganda.

Lesa rejoicing with Martha at the birth of her son Blessing

Topista and Allan cooking seeds for their mushroom project

Pastor Robinah and some ladies sharing the Word of God

11. LOST IN TRANSLATION

The switch between Australia and Uganda has always been an interesting one. As I prepare and countdown to re-entry as I call it, from Australia to Africa, there is always a time of what I call 'my transition period'. This evokes in me many different emotions like excitement, anticipation and sadness at leaving my family once again. It hasn't always been easy but I have no regrets. At times living and working in another country can be a huge challenge and I often found myself at a loss with different emotions erupting in me. From being dirty and dusty, covered in mud at times, depending on the season of weather we were in; to walking or riding a Boda Boda in the pouring rain picking my way through open sewers in slum areas, where people live and work; or standing in line for hours waiting at hospitals, clinics, water, electricity and transport authorities.

Driving a car in Uganda is an experience in itself and definitely not for the faint hearted! There are so many cars on the roads and dirt tracks and the tracks are continually being washed away, new roads constructed and general chaos everywhere. The traffic jams up for hours and hours and all you may move in that time is a couple of kilometres. When the traffic is flowing you need to be able to gently and firmly push your way into oncoming traffic as Bodas, Matatus, bicycles and people whiz past from all different directions.

One of the things I enjoy is riding the Boda Bodas, swerving through the traffic and the people, wind blowing in my face, no helmet, wearing thongs on my feet and having a great chat with the driver as we go. I can't count how many times I've had the most amazing conversations about faith with the driver, mostly always culminating in them humbly asking me to pray for them sometimes resulting in them making a decision to follow Christ with their life.

Early on when we were just starting Treasure Ministries, we got to really know these Boda Boda men well as they were transporting us all over the city every day. Seeing the need for more discipleship teaching we invited them to a meeting. We found a restaurant that was willing to have us and we offered all who came a simple soft drink as that was all we could do. The men came in quiet a large number as they were hungry for this love and compassionate teaching about Jesus and His grace and mercy for all. We sowed good seed back in those days and could see a difference in lives and even though we were unable to continue meeting together, still see the fruit today in the lives we reached out to and touched with a simple love.

A funny incident on a Boda Boda that happened to me is something I refer to as my 'Lost in Translation' story. This particular day Robinah had to go to the Heart Institute at Malago Hospital. I was left at home teaching the English class and when finished I had to close up and make my way to the hospital to meet up with her. I walked up the dirt track to the roadside where I could catch a Boda Boda to Ward 2B at Malago. I jumped on after negotiating a reasonable price with the driver and we were quickly on our way. I asked him if he knew exactly where Ward 2B was at the hospital and he nodded and agreed profusely that he indeed knew where it was and was extremely pleased to be able to deliver me to that exact place. I am quite familiar with Kampala and Malago Hospital so as this young man started to go up some back ways into the hospital, I became a little apprehensive but he assured me that he would be able to get me to where I needed to go. Finally, we arrived and I hopped off, the Boda Boda driver assuring me that we were at Ward 2B.

I waved him off and walked into this unfamiliar area feeling very apprehensive. I spotted people sitting around with white masks over their mouth and nose and as I continued forward there before me was a big sign Tuberculosis Unit. He had indeed delivered me to the TB ward! I was feeling quite sick in the stomach by now as I really had no idea where to go or how to get to where I needed to go as all I could see were sick patients. I spotted some stairs and made my way to them and fortunately some Doctors were on them. I told them my dilemma and they were able to direct me down to where Robinah was waiting for me. This is a classic lost in translation story, especially living in a different language and culture. It's quite humorous now and fortunately I can laugh and cry when these situations occur - which is frequently.

12. BABIES AND JJAJAS

One day as we were visiting and organising the land in the village, we noticed a little girl sitting in the dirt looking very sad and clearly malnourished. She looked old enough to be able to walk but was clearly unable to. We walked over to see her and the old woman and man who seemed to be her carers. Regina was a sad two or three-year-old girl who had been abandoned by her mother and father and left with her grandmother, Jjaja and grandfather who was blind, to care for her. It was obvious that something was wrong with her legs as she had no strength in them to stand. She was definitely at risk of dying if she was left like this. Robinah and I knew that we had to intervene so with permission from the grandparents took her back to Kampala with us to try and help the child.

All of the ladies coming to our classes chose to support Regina's journey back to health. We took her to the local clinic where she was assessed and given medication to de-parasite her and clear her lungs. They also supplied us with a nutritional supplement called Plumpy Nut that we could add to the now different, more nutrient-dense diet we were able to give her. We worked on strengthening her muscles in her legs and getting her walking. We toilet trained her and loved her back to health. Everyone contributed which was absolutely wonderful to see, these ladies who didn't have much themselves, bringing food, clothes and pampers for Regina. Little Regina thrived under this care and within weeks was walking and responding well enough to be able to be returned to her family members. We were able to instruct her Jjaja on the appropriate care for Regina and because she lived close by to us in the village, we were able to check on her frequently. Regina is an active little girl now growing into a beautiful woman with purpose for her life.

Another Jjaja came to us in the village with a week-old baby girl. Her mother had died while giving birth to her because she simply hadn't woken up after the anaesthetic that was administered to her for a caesarean section! The baby was clearly wasting away so we were able to offer help. We loaded up Jjaja who was left to care for her, with bottles, clothes and blankets. Unfortunately, baby formula is just too expensive to be a sustainable help and we were unable to supply this. Living in a village I assumed that there would be a cow or goat to supply the baby with milk. What a mistake it is to assume anything! After checking on the baby a week later it was clear she was dying.

Because of the risk of HIV transmission, no other woman or wet-nurse can nurse another's baby even if the mother has died. The risk of passing it on through the breastmilk is just too great.

Jjaja was feeding her porridge which was maize flour mixed with water into a soupy staple food that most Ugandans eat for breakfast. That is all she had to feed the baby with. After realising our mistake, we went to work quickly and raised enough money to buy a Nanny Goat and her Kid so she could feed the baby fresh goat milk and also have a way to earn a bit of income selling the excess milk in the community.

We were asked to name the beautiful baby and called her Patricia, which means noble. We have kept track of Patricia and her family and it is wonderful to see her thriving and participating in the activities at Treasure Harvest Ministries with her older brothers as they are cared for by grandmother Jjaja.

These children are so at risk in their early years from so many obstacles to their very lives and I can't imagine the number of children who don't make it because there is simply no help and so many mouths to feed. It is survival for the fittest.

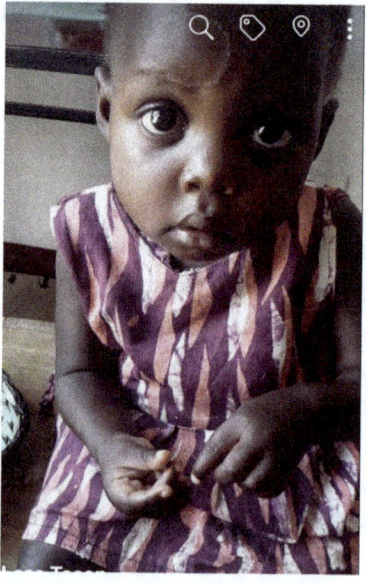

Regina when we first found her and brought her home with us to rehabilitate her

Baby Patricia, who we have looked after from birth

13. WE ARE SLOW BUT WE ARE SURE!

Each time I head back to Africa there is a great work to be done. The responsibility upon me as the ministry grows can be heavy. I need to remember that God doesn't give us anything that we can't handle, He equips us and He is faithful. Leaving behind family and friends leaves me with all kinds of emotional feelings and a definite heightened spiritual awareness of my surroundings and the situations I encounter.

I think anyone truly surrendering to God's will and His calling, especially as they step out in faith, leaving the familiar to embrace the unfamiliar, can leave them feeling a sense of reckless devotion!

By nature, I am a very outgoing, confident risktaker. I also take my responsibility seriously. God has done amazing things in my life and as I step out to serve Him, He continues to take me to new levels of awareness in my relationship with Him. I live to serve Him by loving His children and that is people! It gets messy and dirty and challenging and can be heartbreaking but what an incredible ride this life is. I'm always aware of the frailty of our lives. We are not promised tomorrow so the living needs to happen now, today. Today is the day that we have so make the most of it and press on running the race towards our goal, which is the love of God Himself!

Time seems to go a lot slower in Africa. A favourite saying of Ugandans is, "We are slow but we are sure". Building and construction continued to happen over the years at the ministry site and buildings arose for classes, offices, latrines, dining halls and accommodation for camps and visitors. A huge all-purpose building home for Harvest Church and the many different activities held in it, was built by enthusiastic people from all over the world. This was a huge undertaking for the faithful servants who responded.

I had returned from Uganda with a need for a building to house the ever-growing church and classes held regularly. A wonderful team of people from my home church in Australia responded and started to fundraise and put together a building team to go to Uganda to build an all-purpose building for us. On my return I had the job of organising a cleared space, foundations to be dug and bricks to be made in advance of their arrival. When they did eventually arrive to build, they found that the foundations that I had marked out were a lot bigger than what they had imagined. It seemed like an insurmountable task for them but faithfully they rose to the challenge and over a twelve-month period and two mission trips later, completed an awesome huge, strong building for us which I'm sure will be standing for many years and generations to come! Everything was done with a lot of manual labour, dirty, sweaty and very hard work.

When the pit latrine was dug, the men would just spend days digging by hand and when the hole was so deep, they would just make dents in the walls to pull themselves up as they scrambled up the dirt wall. Amazing to see the hard work and labour put in by so many over the years and the fruit that continues to come and to grow from hearts committed to Jesus.

All the bricks were handmade on site

New church building being built

One of the many buildings going up at Treasure Harvest Ministries

Opening ceremony for Treasure Harvest Ministries in the village of Kaliro Katono

New Church Building

Treasure Dancers performing at the opening of our new church building

14. TEACHING AND CHILD SACRIFICE

In my early days of finding my feet in Uganda I found so many different opportunities to serve. I was teaching creative writing and helping with reading support in a primary school a few days a week. When the school had holidays, another opportunity came about through a conversation with a friend about my desire to work with refugees. My friend got in touch with a Pastor who happened to have a church full of Congolese and Rwandan refugees who spoke French and needed to learn English. The Pastor had been praying for someone to come along to teach them English as they were waiting for relocations into English speaking countries. The call was made at just the right time and we met up the next day and organised for me to start teaching English that week.

I turned up to a tin shed in a slum full of young men and a few women very eager to start learning with their new Teacher Lesa. They were the most eager and delightful students I've ever had the privilege of teaching. I was there at 10am almost every day and we would have the best time of learning, games and fun for hours, sometimes until I couldn't speak anymore! I made wonderful friends through the months that I was able to teach them, learnt a lot about their culture and looked forward to a future, with them and for them as they waited for their futures to unfold.

I was invited to their church to share a message and the title was 'Divine Interruptions'. I talked about the intriguing dynamic of the possibility of God interrupting our lives and plans with His much better plan and how to recognise and take hold of these times turning them into opportunities for good. The refugees and the whole church really received this message well as it touched their hearts. Many of these people were relocated into other countries like America and Australia.

I've had the opportunity to 'move around', as the Ugandans say, while living in Africa. In the early years I went up country and deep into the bush villages to visit and connect with the people living there. I joined a team of health workers surveying people on their knowledge of Malaria, HIV/Aids and maternal health throughout villages in an area called Katakwi in North- Eastern Uganda. What an eye opener into the very real lives of these people and how they live in mud huts, and eat the food they grow and from the livestock they raise.

I have received gifts of gourds, chickens, ground nuts, avocados, pumpkins, mangos, pawpaws, pineapples, passionfruit and bananas and I'm sure a goat as well!

To give food as a gift in Africa is to give life. All other things are useless if you don't have food to eat to survive. This is so different from a western mindset where the more things you have the more prosperous you feel. In reality it is so meaningless and can leave people feeling quite empty inside unless you are giving and using things to be a blessing to others.

A LIFE WORTH LIVING

In my early days in Uganda, I would travel out to the village of Kyampisi to teach the women who lived there English. I worked with an organisation involved in combating the horrific ritual sacrifice and mutilations of children. It is a witch-craft driven problem that involves kidnaps, abduction, torture and murder of children for body parts including ears, tongues, blood and tissue, genitalia and other internal organs. These are then mixed with witch-craft rituals by 'Witch Doctors', to be consumed by spirits that are believed will banish evil, provide prosperity and protection of business, bring good luck and fortune.

It is sickening to see this continuing and I have met many survivors who are maimed for life, like Hope who was abducted and tied to an alter in a shrine at one and a half years old for one year. She was used in rituals, drained of blood, her tongue and teeth cut, and pulled and cut all over her small body. Her body was tossed away when she was of no further use and left to die but was found and rescued and rehabilitated as much as possible by this organisation.

This beautiful little girl can't talk or walk and is confined to a wheelchair but, they couldn't take away her spirit. She is full of glorious smiles and happy laughter and is a living testimony of surviving this evil practice.

Unfortunately, these practises continue to occur but justices are happening.

Distributing clothes in the village

Distributing reusable pads made by our ladies sewing group to girls in a remote village after a lesson on feminine hygiene

15. ADVENTURE IS RISK

I remember one crazy night in Queen Elizabeth National Park. On my way back in to Uganda to minister one time, Robinah and I took a two-day Safari to Queen Elizabeth National Park. The park is Uganda's most popular tourist destination with the Big Five, primates and birds as the attraction.

We left Kampala in the morning traveling by car with the goal of reaching a bush camp by evening at Ishasha where the tree-climbing lions are located. It was late by the time we entered the park and the seventy-kilometre game drive to our destination. About 8pm we were only a couple of kilometres away from the camp when we came across a road block teeming with soldiers. These military men told us that we couldn't pass as rebels from Congo were targeting this stretch of road and taking people. We were very close to the border of Uganda and Congo between Queen Elizabeth and Bwindi National Parks.

A couple of weeks before I had heard on the news that two British tourists had been kidnapped from that area but were released a few days later so I was aware that this was probably not a hoax as anything can happen in Africa. The soldiers directed us to go to a local guesthouse down the road and told us we could stay there overnight and pass in the morning. Honestly my gut feeling was not good but we went and checked out the guesthouse. It was a dubious establishment, loud music playing and people drinking and just not the sort of place that I wanted to stay in so I climbed into the driver's seat turned around and headed back to where the roadblock was. It was getting really late by now and I admit I was feeling scared.

I had heard true stories of groups of militias that were up to no good and had bad intentions so as we neared the group of soldiers, I decided that I was not going to stop. We were just two women so I had to be as bold and as brave as I could be. As the soldiers beckoned me to pull over, I declared loudly that we couldn't stop because people were waiting for us at another lodge! I planted my foot on the accelerator waved goodbye and flashed a convincing smile, and we were off as fast as we could go!

It was so nerve wracking not knowing if we were being chased or not. The adrenaline had kicked in and I was in the fight or flight mode and careening down the dirt road. Only thing was there were herds of elephants dotted everywhere on the dirt road as this is when they come out of the bush to head to the other side, but I was desperate for the toilet. There was only one thing to do, I had to stop between elephant siting's, get out and do my business! My heart was in my mouth but there was nothing else I could do.

We continued driving fast through the bush as I was sure the army was after me. For hours we searched for a lodge or a camp to stay at. This is the 'Big 5' country and we were amongst them. After getting quite lost in some tall grass looking for a place to stay, we came across a sign for a lodge and pulled up to a locked gate and no sign of life. After honking the horn to alert someone that we were there and assuring them of who we were, the staff let us in. It was actually a lovely place and the staff were so hospitable and welcoming that we ended up staying there for two nights and enjoying a safari the next day spotting all the animals we had come to see. It was a great ending to what could have been a very different story.

These are the highlights of living in a beautiful country like Uganda. The opportunities to visit the many different National Parks and to see the animals living in the wild.

I would often go for a short safari to Murchison Park as this park was close to where the Ministry base was. Murchison Falls National Park is Uganda's largest and oldest conservation area hosting 76 species of mammals and over 450 birds. The park is bisected by the Victoria Nile and the dramatic Murchison Falls where the Nile squeezes through an 8m wide gorge and plunges with a thunderous roar into the 'Devil's Cauldron', creating a beautiful trademark rainbow. The wildlife in the park is amazing and includes Elephants, Giraffes and Buffaloes, and at the river, Hippos, Nile crocodiles and aquatic Birds.

There are great rest camps to stay at that are close to the river crossing and Budongo Forest is a great place to go chimp trekking in. To get up close to these amazing animals is a fantastic experience. I've seen a Hyena scavenging on a leftover carcass after a Lion had finished eating, a Pumba [warthog] family and a herd of Elephants coming to a waterhole to refresh themselves as well as trekking a family of Chimpanzee in a forest and being able to sit quietly as part of the group and observe them in their territory - absolutely amazing.

One thing that is very frustrating for me about living in Uganda is how slow everything can be. So many times I have been stuck in cafes waiting for the car to be fixed or the rain to stop or to be picked up. I try to always have something with me to occupy time but for a productive person like me this can be a time of testing! I'm sure my patience has been drawn to ultimate levels so many times.

16. JIGGERS AND OTHER DELIGHTS

I had returned to Uganda to do some building and overseeing work on some new buildings and somehow, I had picked up a Jigger in my foot. Jiggers unfortunately are a part of life in Uganda, especially those living in rural areas and with close contact to animals as most do.

A Jigger is a parasitic flea that burrows into the skin, especially the feet, and can cause extreme pain. If not removed from the body, they can cause it to rot. I've known of cases where children and adults have been infested with hundreds of Jiggers causing crippling circumstances in their lives. Fortunately, there are organisations wholly devoted to removing these from those people in need of help.

As for me I had one Jigger in my toe, probably picked up in the dirt from a game park or from our farm and it needed to be removed. I sterilized a safety pin and Robinah used it to remove it and then cut the skin around the wound for what she said was quick healing. It was a very painful experience for me and very funny for the Ugandans watching the extraction and laughing at the mzungu who got a Jigger in her foot. Somehow this made me feel like a real African. Over the years unfortunately I do seem to pick up a jigger or two, one of the joys of living in the bush and visiting people in their mud homes. It's a small annoyance compared to the joy of sharing their lives and loving them.

Oh, the joys of driving in Uganda. Apparently, the rule is to push your way in, hope that no one hits you and pray that you will reach your destination without killing anyone or being killed yourself. The traffic police, usually very large women dressed in stiff white uniforms or tall ferocious looking men in the same uniform, are notorious for wanting bribes.

Once when I was driving in Kampala, in the confusion of traffic every which way I looked, I turned into a one-way street with absolutely no traffic on it, thinking I had found a reprieve from the chaos all around. Robinah realised the mistake I had made and directed me to turn around and to make a quick exit back to where I had come from. Unfortunately, the traffic policeman dressed in his white uniform had spotted me and was blowing his whistle and waving his arms wildly at me gesturing for me to pull over. I had no option but to do as he said. Apparently, I had broken the law and driven down the presidential way, that only President Musevini himself was allowed to use. I had committed a terrible crime and was being severely chastised for it! He had me sit on the side of the road and kept telling me I would have to go to the local police station and to court as well! I was trying to explain that I had made a mistake and could he find it in his heart to forgive me. Really what he wanted from me was a bribe and I knew it.

Thankfully Robinah talked to the man while I furiously prayed for a solution, explaining that because she was unwell, I was driving for her in this unfamiliar part of Kampala and that she would take all the blame for the mistake I had made. The policeman softened as we shared our work and hearts with him and eventually, he let us go with a warning. Amazingly he was full of smiles, almost a completely different man than what we had first encountered.

On another occasion we were stopped multiple times for no reason other than to check registration and licence. Somebody had taken the numbers of our rego and written them on someone else's misdemeanour. This is an inside job, part of the corruptness in the police force. We have had to get to the bottom of this which takes a lot of time and effort being connected to the right person in the right office but eventually we have proven ourselves to be in the right and the charges were let go. It's so wrong and so corrupt but God has been faithful to us and led us to the right people to be able to help and sort out the mess.

Traffic lights have sprung up everywhere in Kampala but many motorists don't know how to use them. After so many years of driving freestyle and anything goes, people just won't stop at red lights and will not wait till the light goes green before taking off, causing absolute chaos all around them. The Boda Bodas sail through the red lights with their passengers clinging on, reading or talking on their mobile phones. Overcrowded Matatus think they have right of way on all roads and continually zip past, pushing in and causing all kinds of near misses and traffic violations everywhere.

There are countless numbers of 'saloons' across this country. A saloon is a hairdressing salon and it seems everyone needs one. These small shops are full of clients from morning till late into the night. Children and men wear their hair short, clipped and shaved to almost bald. Most school children attending school adhere to the government regulation of hair short and shaved for hygiene and cleanliness and also so there is no comparison or competition between students.

Women on the other hand love their weaves! These types of hair extensions or hair pieces come in all colours, shapes and sizes. No one really knows what they are made from when you ask but they are usually synthetic fibres glued or sewn onto natural hair. The Ugandan women use the term 'I'm going to the saloon to plant my hair!' Afterwards they leave this weave or wig in for weeks and weeks and inevitably the hand patting on the head starts. I believe this is to alleviate the itch that develops as the scalp gets dirtier, or it could be any manner of things hiding under there! The process can take hours. The natural hair is separated into parts and the fibre attached to the hair and braided into the hair into the style that the person wants. One to many people go to work on the hair depending how quickly it needs to be done. Usually, it takes a long time resulting in a very happy lady who feels like a glamorous model walking out of the saloon and into the dusty, dirty streets and slums of the town.

This is a skill we have taken on board in our vocational school, to teach local women so they too can start a business generating an income for themselves which in turn helps their family and the wider community.

I've had a lot of fun purchasing dummy heads of hair in downtown Kampala for our classes to practise on. One of the things I really enjoy about this ministry is the wide variety of activities I get to do and the hands-on things I participate in daily, from greeting and teaching children at our school, teaching a variety of classes to adults, harvesting coffee on the property, digging in the garden, intervention in crises as they occur, attending formal meetings and preaching a message in a church, as well as the occasionally taking people on safari moments. All in a day's work here at Treasure Harvest Ministries.

Ladies in sewing lessons

Handing out mattresses to very needy families. Most kids have never had a mattress to sleep on.

17. KALIRO KATONO

Living in the village of Kaliro Katono has been a lovely experience, so different to living in the densely populated capital city of Kampala.

Kaliro Katono actually means 'small fire'. Originally the village was known as Kiranyi and was named after a well-known wealthy man who had many wives and lots of children. When the village was small a man came and built a small shop and as there was no electricity then, he would keep a small candle lit in the doorway. As darkness descended so people would be able to see to make their way to the shop. The vendor was sure that even though these were small beginnings, the town would become bigger and the fire would spread.

The area was also a target for the military to come and recruit young people into their armed forces.

Kaliro Katono today is a thriving trading centre and home to many families that have lived in the same place for years diligently working their land and businesses. The air is fresh and void of the burning smoke from heaped piles of rubbish and plastic everywhere in the city. The days are peaceful and full of the pleasant noises of birds singing, roosters crowing and the laughter of children as they play. There is a lot of activity in the village as people rise early to go to work in their gardens, digging and planting food. Usually this is a whole family affair with even the small children accompanying and participating in the work.

Ugandans are quiet busy people, not opposed to hard work. If families have the money for school fees, the children are in school but due to certain circumstances more often than not a lot of children are not in school.

Vivian was a young 14-year-old girl who started to come to Harvest Church from the beginning when we met under the mango tree. She lived with her grandmother as both her parents had died of Aids. Vivian would turn up all the time desperately asking for help to go back to school. I went with Robinah to Vivian's home and to meet her grandmother to see how we could help. There were a lot of family members in the house so it can be hard to know what really is going on but Jjaja assured us that there was no one to pay Vivian's school fees at that time and she was simply unable to send her back. After some discussion with them both we were willing to pay the fee for her to return to school for that term. This means that I have to raise this money somehow and at that stage it would have to come from me. It is so sad to see these children having to rely on their caregivers for support when the person is just unable to do it financially.

It really impacts your life as a person who has had a completely different upbringing being nurtured and cared for, educated in the best learning environments and never having to worry or even think about having enough food to eat or clothes to wear or being sent to school.

Unfortunately, so many girls like Vivian, if there is no intervention, are forced into early marriages or any sort of work like a maid or even prostitution that will help them survive.

We continued with our classes of sewing, beading, hairdressing and English lessons so we could give as many people as possible, especially women, some skills to help them become independent and start their own small business. Irene, our sewing teacher from Kampala, would come out to the village once a week to teach the women. We were able to gift a sewing machine to Irene which enabled her to start her own business, earning income.

Robinah taught the ladies to make paper bead jewelry, but there was not much interest in the village as there was nowhere to sell it and the local people didn't have a need for jewelry. I woud take what they made me when I returned to Australia to sell, as well as bags that the sewing women had made. The proceeds went straight back to the ladies.

I continued to teach English classes whenever I was in Uganda. These were well attended by young adults.

We have helped these people to become better equipped for living and working in the village, and those who have headed to the bigger towns and cities for work.

18. WITCHCRAFT IN UGANDA

The Lugandan term for witchcraft is Busamiize. One of the oldest cultural traditions is twin initiation. If twins are born in the Buganda tribe they must be initiated into the clan. The belief is that behind the twins is special power. The children around them grow up with the belief that if they annoy or make an enemy of a twin, the twin could put a curse on them. When the twins are born a basket is placed under each baby's head. The baskets are filled by the family members with money, eggs, coffee, seeds and shells. The clan members offer up the basket to evil spirits. If anything is stolen from this basket by a person it can result in an accident or anything leading to death for them. If one of the twins dies, it is said that he or she has disappeared or flown to heaven.

The initiation ceremony happens with all the clan members present. The maternal grandfather stands and people shout obscene words at him. The mother-in-law and the father of the twins stand and dance while beating their own buttocks. The umbilical cord from both babies, which has been kept, is placed into a basket filled with water. If the cords rise to the top of the water these twins are of that clan. If not, it means the babies belong to another clan. This means the father is not really the father and the twins may die immediately.

The initiation involves 'Tying'- Okusiiba. When the twins are tied, if a snake or insect like a butterfly comes into the shrine the animal is captured and tied in bark cloth and a string of local white beads is tied and draped around the parents. The next morning the parents move back to the shrine where food has been prepared. They place the food on their heads and the grandparents join them, also placing the food on their heads. If the food falls at the front of the shrine the father's side of the family have to prepare a goat at the shrine for eating. After everyone has eaten, a non-clan member, but still in the family, places his or her foot in the food and the non-clan members are able to eat.

If the twins don't survive birth, the mother places butter on a knife and inserts it into a banana tree. The next morning if the new growth has started to die the twins are of the father's clan, if not then he is not the father. This is the Buganda tribal cultural practice, the people living in central Uganda.

There are many different tribal customs still going on all over Uganda and Africa. Living in a village in the bush surrounded by shrines and traditional ways has opened my eyes to the very presence of darkness in the lives of people. Many family members have come to Treasure Harvest Ministries seeking a way out of the bondage and evil that is happening in their lives. We always point them to Jesus Christ the saviour as the answer.

Paul was experiencing demonic attacks in his family home not far from our place where his children were getting sick and there was no peace. Odd things were happening to him and he was visited regularly by evil spirits. The family decided to call a witchdoctor in for help to get rid of these spirits. The witchdoctor came after he had extracted an exorbitant amount of money from the family and did some witchcraft. He was beaten up and told Paul that he could not help in this case and that they were certainly going to die. Next Paul called in the Catholic Priest as he had a background in Catholicism but the priest and nuns could not help either as nothing changed.

Paul used to see Robinah and I walk past his home early in the morning and knew us as the 'born agains'. He wanted to approach us but was too scared to try. But God had a plan. We needed some concreting work done at this time and got in contact with our usual workman. He was busy on another job but promised to send his offsider with help to complete the work. Paul was the help and he found himself coming to work at Treasure Ministries. After several days he got up the courage to approach Robinah and share his story with her and to ask if she could help! Robinah went with Paul to his home that very afternoon and shared with his whole extended family the good news of Jesus Christ and how he had come to earth and died for our sins so that we could be forgiven and have a relationship of freedom with God. Paul, his wife and children all surrendered their lives to God right then and there. There were no more incidents with evil, Paul's children got better and they started to attend every meeting and event at Harvest Church and the ministry. Their lives were completely changed and now they walked in freedom and victory.

19. TRAVELLING IN EAST AFRICA

In 2016 I had an amazing opportunity to visit Ethiopia and to fulfil a dream of going to visit The Hamlin Fistula Hospital in Addis Ababa, started by Reg and Catherine Hamlin to help women injured from complications in childbirth.

Addis Ababa is a wet and rainy, damp city, home to millions of people and a lot of beggars but on the outskirts next to a river is this beautiful little hospital devoted to helping women all over Ethiopia suffering from fistulas.

An obstetric fistula is a hole between the vagina and rectum or bladder that is caused by prolonged obstructed labour, leaving a woman incontinent of urine or faeces or both. It most commonly occurs among women who live in low-resource countries, who give birth without access to medical help. If a woman's labour becomes obstructed, she could remain in excruciating pain for days before her baby is dislodged. Her baby usually dies and she is left with a fistula and often rejected by her husband and village due to her foul smell.

The Hamlin's have dedicated their lives to helping these women and have teaching hospitals and trained midwifes all over Ethiopia. Dr Catherine was still living at the hospital in Addis and I had the privilege of touring through the hospital, meeting and interacting with the patients, seeing first hand how the recovery process happens and just having a peer into the lives of these women. The grounds were so pretty and kept immaculate all helping towards the healing of these precious women. The women participated in craft and sewing throughout their healing as well as physio and exercise to strengthen them before returning home. Unfortunately, some women were left in a way that they were unable to return to their homes but they were able to be housed at the villages set up for them. This was hope in the middle of such terrible suffering. I didn't get to meet Dr Catherine who was in her nineties at the time but was thrilled and honoured to see the great work that had been done and was still happening.

We left Addis to tour the Southern Omo Valley. Home to many traditional and ancient, cultural tribes of people that were living the same way as they had done for centuries beforehand.

The Konso tribal people lived in villages cut into stone on the side of a mountain. Trekking into the village and walking around was amazing. Our guide showed us the many traditional houses made from mud and grass and enclosed by stone walls. Also the raised large hut where the boys, once they reached a certain age, all slept together before initiation into manhood.

They were agriculturalists and grew cotton and the women were beautifully dressed in long dresses locally woven. There were wooden statues all around representing deceased important family members and heroic events. There was a public gathering spot for ceremonies, rituals, dances, food preparations and weaving. Outside the village was an enormous eroding plateau composed of hoodoo landforms, slender and tall spires of rock protruding from the base of an arid drainage basin formation known as 'Konso New York City', a fabulous tourist attraction to the area. We had such fun walking through the village built into the stony cliffs interacting with the children and welcoming adults.

Then we were off to see the Dorze people, also expert weavers and renowned builders of towering huts resembling giant beehives. They are agriculturalists and small-scale farmers growing cotton and maize and distilling their own alcoholic beverage. We watched the preparation of Kotcho [flat bread] out of the trunk of Enset, false banana, and at a small ceremony tasted the home brewed liquor with the men of the tribe, drinking to our good health all in good fun building relations and friendship with the people. We tried out the hand weaving and spinning and observed these master craftsmen at work weaving cloths and blankets. I got to try my culinary skills at making Kotcho from scratch, grinding the flour and cooking the bread over coals and then eating it. These beautiful people were so hospitable and a delight to be amongst.

The Mursi tribe are one of the most fascinating still adhering to their traditional and unique culture. The Mursi women wore clay or wooden plates many as large as saucers in their lower lips or earlobes. These are to mark rites of passages and they start wearing them around fifteen years old. The women are famous for their unique headdresses made from colourful beads, seeds, animal skins, tusks and metal rings. Adorning themselves with jewellery is very important to them. They have an ancient way of bartering and sharing goods with each other and the men have a stick fighting ceremony which is a ritualised form of violence. I was able to purchase my very own lip plate from these amazing people and they led me around their village, everyone touching or holding on to me as if not to let me go. Personal space is really non-existent in tribal life as everyone does everything together!

Then we were off to see the extraordinary Hamer people with their unique expression and culture. We arrived just as the women were returning from the bull jumping ceremony that marked a rite of passage for men and initiated boys into manhood. The ceremony had begun with all the female relatives performing a dance and offering themselves to be whipped by the men showing their support to the initiate and giving them a right to demand his help in a time of need. Then the men had to jump over eight bulls in order to be allowed to marry.

We were now invited to be part of the celebration at the end where lots of traditional food was being prepared and cooked. The funny thing was that all the girls were wearing western bras. As I connected with the girls, they told me that they welcomed the whipping as it was all part of them being able to get married and this was very important to being accepted as part of the tribe. The men were wearing a clay cap that was painted and decorated with feathers and ornaments on their heads. The Hamer have a distinctive hairstyle that involves curling the hair with a mixture of butter and ochre clay and their huts that they live in have a similar shape. So, as you can imagine we came across some interesting smells!

Meeting the Dassanech people was fascinating. Dassanech means 'People of the Delta'. We had to canoe across the Omo River to where they live on the banks of the river. The land is semi-arid and extremely dry. It was like a desert and so hot. They built round houses from rusty corrugated iron sheets, rope, animal skins and trees. Some women were making a new house from scratch when we arrived so we were able to observe and interact with the ladies. They had livestock, mainly cattle and goats, and the men would hunt crocodile and occasionally small hippopotamus and fish in the river in their small dugout canoes. This was the harshest of lands where female circumcision was still practised, drought, disease and raids from other tribes threatened their existence daily.

I remember Robinah making a funny comment at this time about thanking God that she hadn't been born here! It truly was an eye-opening experience to the ways of life around the world. As we continued to travel through the villages in rural Ethiopia, we stopped to see the people in their homes. They were very welcoming inviting us inside to see how they lived and we watched the women making Injera, the fermented sourdough-risen flatbread that is eaten with everything. It is traditionally made out of Teff flour which has a spongy texture and is the national dish. As we continued on the road donkeys were everywhere pulling carts full of Teff and families or carrying loads of the grain, so that all you could see was four legs and a nose coming out of this mound of golden grain.

Ethiopia is a huge country full of ancient rock-cut churches, tombs and castles. There were museums and interesting finds everywhere but my heart was to meet with and interact with the people.

A LIFE WORTH LIVING

Visiting different tribes

In Ethiopia with a woman from the Omo valley tribes

In Ethiopia with girls who had just come from a bull jumping initiation for boys to become men

Pastor Robinah in Ethiopia with Omo Valley tribeswomen

20. HANGING OUT IN EAST AFRICA

I've also had opportunities to travel to and tour Rwanda many times and to explore this 'Land of a Thousand Hills'. It is a beautiful country with a landscape made up of many rolling hills, a clean environment, a rich culture, plenty of wildlife and welcoming people. Kigali the capital had a very French flavour, even cobblestone streets in places, and the French patisseries were delicious. I travelled to Lake Kivu, one of Africa's great lakes, and to the towns of Gisenye and Kibuye.

I travelled down the Congo Nile Trail squashed into a Matatu - taxi, with about twenty people for hours, only stopping for toilet stops in the most precarious places. I was even vomited on by one of the sick passengers on this trip. Definitely not for the faint hearted! At the end of the trail we climbed onto the back of two motorbikes and journeyed well into the night to arrive at a monastery turned into a backpacker's lodge. Perched high on a mountain, it overlooked beautiful Lake Kivu and the Congo. The hospitality is amazing in these out of the way places and the people so friendly. The church attached to the monastery had a memorial place filled with the skulls of people who had been slaughtered in the genocide of 1994.

I have visited the Genocide Memorial in Kigali a number of times, which honours the memory of the more than one million Rwandans killed in the 1994 genocide through education and peace-building. Each visit has been an extremely moving experience helping me to understand the events leading up to the senseless mass slaughter of a people.

Once Robinah and I travelled by local bus deep into a village in Rwanda to visit her grandfather on her mother's side and some family members who were getting married. After a frighteningly fast and furious drive through the hills and around sharp corners on dirt roads, we were dropped off and proceeded to the village on the back of a motorbike.

We reached the place where the family were preparing for an introduction. This is when the bride and grooms' families come together and the bride-to-be introduces her future husband to her friends, parents and relatives. The ceremony was outside in the bush with everyone sitting around on plastic chairs and wooden benches with a man speaking on behalf of the couple. Baskets were filled with money which was the bride price which has the purpose of validating and legitimising the relationship between the man and woman. There were people arriving on foot and wheeling bicycles carrying food of all descriptions for the party afterwards. Towards the end of the formalities large flasks with straws were passed around containing a local brew of alcohol for all to enjoy. We were then invited to come inside the house to eat the food that was served to everyone. Afterwards there was music and traditional dancing with much laughter and fun. We also had the opportunity to share with the members of the family of God's love for them. Several people responded by surrendering their lives to Jesus which brought great joy to all of us and made our journey to this remote place so worthwhile. I should mention that I was the first white person to visit this place that anyone could remember!

When we were staying on Lake Kivu at Gisenye we would walk to the beach for a swim in the lake and always end up with lots of young boys and men joining us and having fun, all curious to know all about us. We would make friends easily and share the Gospel with them and they responded in a wonderful way. The people are so open to the love of God and willing to hear, understand and respond to the opportunity to know their Father in Heaven and the grace and love He wants to pour out on them.

We would walk to the border crossing between Rwanda and Congo at the town of Goma, meeting interesting characters along the way through the markets where colourful kitenge material wraps were sold as well as every other conceivable household object, building utensils and second-hand clothes and shoes were offered for a price. There were so many people everywhere all the time and it was easy to be distracted by the chaotic ways of life around me. Tall slender women carried huge loads on their heads and men were busy pushing wheelbarrows and building or working on roads. The culture in rural Rwanda was very different than the city life of Kigali where there were a lot of young students and workers, all dressed immaculately, hurrying from one place to another. The streets were clean and tidy and there seemed to be order. In fact I was told that you could get harassed by police for wearing the shower thongs that were provided at guesthouses and places of accommodation to you outside. In other words, it was quite formal and you needed to dress respectfully in the culture.

Most Africans dress formally with shirts, pants, jackets and shoes for men and the women in long dresses or skirts and blouses and heeled shoes or colourful kitenge made dresses, while jeans are culturally accepted and worn by the youth now. It is important to 'look smart', especially when attending functions, ceremonies or church.

Kenya is a favourite place to visit for me, especially over on the coast near Mombasa. I have travelled by bus from Kampala spending all day and night right through to Nairobi, and taken a train to Mombasa. It is an awesome opportunity to really see and be immersed in the landscape when traveling through the Rift Valley that divides Kenya down the length, the highlands and low plains and National Parks. I love seeing the beautiful Baobab trees, the houses and homes, and the ways people live along the way, while spotting animals like Zebra and Elephants.

Arriving in Nairobi in the early hours of the morning while it's still dark can be chaotic and frightening. There is usually a room at the bus company's destination that you can wait in till it is light and safe to venture out onto the streets.

It's always so good when I travel with Robinah to these places as there is safety in numbers and two heads can work better than one, especially when you have luggage that if you take your eyes off for a second is gone, and you really need to pee.

We made our way over to Mombasa on the Indian Ocean, Kenya's oldest city. From there decided whether to go north or south. Both beautiful destinations. Diani is a coastal holiday place where there is plenty of action on the beach. Fisherman returning from fishing trips with a catch of octopus which they proceed to throw against the beach sand to prepare and tenderise before cooking. There are camel rides on offer and many Maasai men walking the beach looking for opportunities, especially of the single white female kind!

Being the friendly, exuberant person that I am and truly interested in the Maasai culture, I've had a few propositions of marriage - which I just laugh off.

To the north is the town of Malindi and the beachside Italian influenced smaller town of Watamu. It is a peaceful village nestled between pristine beaches and rainforest with access to the very interesting ancient ruins of Gedi, a medieval Swahili-Arab settlement.

A bus or a train ride through this incredible country helped me to appreciate the diverse landscape from the dry barren plains dotted with huge Baobab and Acacia trees to the coastline and the amazing Sisal fibre crops with their sword-shaped leaves north of Mombasa and the many marine parks along the coast.

One birthday I had on the island of Zanzibar off the coast of Tanzania. I had had an old postcard with a picture of fisherman from Zanzibar on it that I'd picked up in a café somewhere years beforehand and placed it in the door pocket in my old Subaru. I would get it out from time to time over the years and dream, speaking out that I would one day visit this exotic Spice Island, as it was known as. Sure enough, I found myself on a plane bound for Dar Es Salaam, a major city of Tanzania.

When we alighted from the plane, we were to look for Hajj, a little old Muslim man who would be our contact to drive us to a safe guesthouse for the night before catching the ferry over to Zanzibar the next day. What an interesting and fun time we had with him as we looked around the city and walked through the markets with all the exotic foods on display.

Hajj dropped us off at a safe, affordable guesthouse for the night with a promise to return first thing the next day to take us to catch the Kilimanjaro fast ferry across to Zanzibar. The ferry we caught was built by an Australian boat builder so that intrigued me but not as much as the hundreds of people we were lined up with to trying to purchase tickets.

Tanzania is predominantly a Muslim country and it just so happened that it was the month of Ramadan, a time of fasting and prayer for Muslims. Many people were returning to their homes on Zanzibar to celebrate with family. After a very choppy crossing we alighted and made our way to Stone Town. Once again, we met an interesting and very helpful guide who drove us to Stone Town and helped us secure good affordable accommodation for a couple of nights. Wandering through the lanes and streets of this ancient place, with ornate houses built with local stone by Arab traders and slavers years, before was so surreal! The history was evident and it is estimated that around 600,000 slaves were sold through Zanzibar in the 1800s. We visited several sites where these poor people had been chained and held before being sold. It was devastating, ugly and a sad reminder for me of what we are capable of.

We left Stone Town after celebrating my birthday and travelled up the coast to one of the beautiful beachside guesthouses where we stayed for a few wonderous filled days walking the beach, immersing with the local people, watching the fisherman in their Dhows hauling in their catch and swimming in the warm clear waters of the Indian Ocean. It was in fact Robinah's first time to see and swim in an ocean. She was a big hit with the local Maasai population, and they called her Rasta Pastor because of the dreads in her hair and they just loved her. This gave us lots of opportunity to share about Christ with these fascinating, gentle people.

It's probably always a fascinating thing to many people to see the interaction between Robinah and I because we are true sisters in every sense of the word yet we look and act so differently. I've had many comments made to me over the years about the love and care that we show to one another and so hopefully people realise that it's God's love in action shown through two very different people from different cultures. I've had to laugh as people even think that I am Robinah's mum!

We toured as much of the Spice Island as we could on our budget. The spice tour was very interesting, seeing how all the different spices were grown and making hats and carry bags out of Banana fibre as part of the tour. I always like to support the little businesses by buying the product on offer and this time it was lots of lovely spices!

When I travel into these countries and in fact whenever I travel anywhere I rarely pre book any accommodation etc. but prefer to wing it and see what is on offer and make my choice then. I realise this can be risky but the surprises, adventures and divine appointments have been so worth it. I really do walk by faith and not by sight totally relying on God to lead me in the unknown.

Leaving Zanzibar on the ferry was quite a feat. It was a very choppy journey back to the mainland with rolling seas and poor Robinah not being used to travel on the sea was so ill, continually bringing up all the food she had consumed in the past few days on the Island. The whole Island experience was wonderful and an experience I definitely will repeat.

21. EVIL SPIRITS IN THE VILLAGE

Progress at the ministry site continued in amazing ways as building after building popped up. Teams from Australia and Germany came to build not only physical buildings but to input, encourage and build into people's lives.

A large all-purpose building was built over a two-phase period of time with the foundations and slab being built first then the bricks being hand made on site and then a year later the actual building was constructed. A tremendous effort was put in by people from all over the world from fundraising to finish, with many people being blessed then and for generations to come.

At the same time, we had a team of people come from Australia to run a children's camp for vulnerable kids from the village. This was an impacting time for all involved which resulted in changed lives for the better and a realisation throughout the village and surrounds that they were loved, people were caring for them and their lives mattered. They were not forgotten people.

With the increase came responsibility to be good stewards of the facilities and the accompanying growth. Better organised vocational classes emerged and Hairdressing was added to the already established Tailoring and other classes.

A LIFE WORTH LIVING

Emma was an engineer by trade. Married to Lukea, they had five young children between them. Emma's parents had both died when he was in Senior 3 at school, equivalent to Grade 10 in Australia. He had a Catholic upbringing but had no real relationship with God. He'd had a past relationship with a girl who was jealous of his relationship with Lukea and so was thought to be practising witchcraft towards Emma and his family.

It was discovered that she was paying a witchdoctor to bring harm to Lukea. Emma was desperate to cancel the spirits coming against his wife so he went to a witchdoctor. Emma set about selling his assets to raise the money required by the witchdoctor to help him.

Lukea was suffering hallucinations, being terrorised and was starting to lose her mind. The whole family were living in a state of terror. Emma went to the Catholic charismatics for help but even they were scared and nothing changed. Emma lost opportunities for work and there seemed to be no favour upon his life, only increasing despair. He knew about us because we walked by his house everyday but he was afraid to approach us for help.

God has a way of working things out. Robinah needed a skilled worker to start on some buildings for the school we had in mind so she called our usual builder who just happened to have a job he was working on and was unable to come so he sent his friend Emma to us.

Robinah was able to share the life, love and work of Jesus with Emma, who in turn repented and accepted Jesus into his life and was saved. Robinah went to Emma's home and shared with all of his extended family. They prayed together, Lukea and the children accepting Jesus Christ as their Lord and saviour. The demonic attacks completely stopped.

Favour returned to this family's life as they changed their lives to serve Jesus and share His transforming love with friends and other people.

Once a month in the village the neighbours hold a ceremony at night using traditional drums and calling out to the spirits to come. The people participating go into a trance like state, are naked and do what the demons tell them to do. They also use animal blood to paint their bodies.

Alice was living in a small mud house with a rusty iron sheet roof with her five children and father of the children. She lived in abject poverty, digging daily in a garden just to get something for them to eat. Her seven-year-old daughter had just died from suspicious circumstances. People were saying it was from malaria but Alice was beginning to realize the truth. In fact, the whole village was suspecting that witchcraft was at hand. Her two-year-old had died in previous years in the same way. Her seven-year-old daughter had come home from school sick with fever. Alice left to fetch water from the well leaving the father of the child in charge. While Alice was gone her teenage daughter arrived home to find her sister nearly dead and pleaded with her father to take her to the hospital. The father refused and tragically the young girl died. Alice and the entire village mourned the death and loss of this precious child.

As time went on Alice became aware of her husband's dabbling in witchcraft because of his hunger for wealth and power. Demonic spirit attacks frequented this family and this precious young girl was the innocent victim of child sacrifice!

Through intervention Treasure Harvest Ministries has been able to work with this family and to enrol the youngest child into our nursery school for vulnerable children. When I first met this little boy, I honestly thought he was not going to live into adulthood. Today he is thriving in every way just because someone cared enough to do something about his circumstances.

Organising a hot water system for visiting teams on top of the latrine Ugandan style

Children's dancing group performing in a Harvest Church service

Kiddies performing in a skit at children's camp

22. CATHIE LEE NURSERY SCHOOL

One of my great desires has been to start a school for vulnerable children here in Uganda. A school that has the very best education, giving each person a foundation of positive thinking, respect for others and a confidence in God's love. I believe children need to be taught how to think independently and be clear about ideas and beliefs that form the foundation of their lives. They need to focus on ideas and morals that relate to everyone like truth and honour, justice and purity, righteousness and excellence.

So, in 2019 we prepared to open a nursery school on site for a class of 3 to 4-year-old vulnerable children from the village. There was a lot of preparation involved with a lot of legal requirements to do. We had a long list to attend to from plans for the buildings, setting up and equipping the classrooms and outdoor play areas, building a school kitchen to feed the kids and staff, registering the school with all of the different departments involved and finding the right kids to register.

We really wanted to give the opportunity to children from the most vulnerable and needy families, those children that were being overlooked, cared for by grandparents because their own parents had died or abandoned them, single parent families and kids who were malnourished and simply not being looked after adequately.

When we had set the opening date, we informed the church members and told them to inform the neediest families they knew. Soon there was a steady stream of people arriving with small children to ask for an interview to see if their child qualified for a position at the new school. We heard very sad stories of families in desperate situations, just begging us for the opportunity to have at least one of their children enrolled in the school.

Thirtyfour year-old Zebeeda came to us early one morning carrying her three year-old daughter Margaret, who had been severely burnt over her entire stomach and legs as her dress had caught alight when she went too close to the cooking fire. She had to leave Margaret and her twin sister at home in the care of her not much older brothers and sisters as she went to look for firewood so the family could cook their food. The child was in a terrible way and Zebeeda was hopelessly crying in desperation. She had no money and 8 children to care for. She said that she wanted to take her own life because it was just too much to bear on her own anymore.

We went into immediate action sending her and her daughter to a medical clinic nearby where she could access treatment for the badly burned child, while we went to a market to buy fresh supplies of essential food for the family. We took the food over to where she lived and to check on the other children. We were able to see for ourselves the conditions in which the family were living. Then we alerted the people in our church who organised a support system for her. Together we checked daily on the family, bringing food relief, medication, social and mental support so they did not feel alone in this crisis time.

A LIFE WORTH LIVING

Zebeeda was born near the small village of Kalule close to Kaliro Katona, one of seven children to farming parents. All the children were sent to primary school while their mother was alive due to her efforts to give her children the best start in life but sadly, she died when Zebedda was in Primary 6, so that was the end of her education.

Her father remarried, as is the case in most families in Uganda, because of the need for someone to look after his kid. But the stepmother was not too fond of her new stepchildren so Zebeeda reached out for love and acceptance in other places. She found herself pregnant and having her first child at the tender age of seventeen, followed quickly by other children. Her firstborn a girl Lukea was a normal child making all the right milestones. At one and a half she was subjected to witchcraft, stopped speaking and was deaf by the age of three. Zebeeda's marriage was abusive and violent and her husband threatened to burn her and the children in the house. Zebeeda had to leave him immediately and she went to Sudan to find work to start again, leaving her kids with her sister-in-law. Zebeeda met another man, fell pregnant and had twin girls Margaret and Pauline. She thought he loved her and wanted the family and he did help for four months and then fled.

Zebeeda was on her own once again with seven children to care for. She returned to Kalule and rented a small room for herself and the children. Once again, a man came and left, leaving Zebeeda pregnant with her eighth child Martin.

Because of our intervention at a very critical time and Zebeeda's determination and hard work, five of her children are in school. Lukea is attending a deaf school where they have even given her a cow to look after and the firstborn calf is hers to keep. She can earn some money from the cow and it also gives her status in the community which, being deaf, she would not have otherwise.

The family live in meagre dwellings, two brick rooms and a dirt floor that we were able to finish with concrete and get a solar panel to run three lights. They cook outside over a wood fire with only a few pots, there is no refrigerated storage, their shower and toilet are outside and used by the other people living in the buildings next to them. It is day to day living preparing a meal with what is grown in the garden and the generosity of others that have excess food to share with the family. They live in extreme poverty compared even to others around them but slowly this is changing with love and support from THM.

The twins are enrolled in Cathie Lee Nursery School with full support which eases her burden of good education for her children and is a safe place for them to be, with fee support for the others.

Her plan for their future is to start a small business to bring income in to raise her family. Zebeeda's vision for her family is to provide each child with a good education to break the despairing cycle of poverty, to own her own land and to build a good house to live in. Zebeeda would like to start a hair, beauty and design saloon where she can use the creative gifts God has given her. She tries to explain how she feels about Treasure Harvest Ministries, thanking God for working through this ministry to give her life, freedom and hope in Jesus for her future. She comes from a Muslim family but chose to follow Christ when she was 14 years old. She knows she has made many mistakes and bad choices but admits God has always been with her and has not forsaken her.

Zebeeda and lots of other women and men struggle to survive every day and provide for their families. But with love and support from dedicated people around her now, she understands that she is now part of a larger family where she feels included and is not alone. This plays a tremendous part in healing and experiencing wellbeing while navigating life in rural Uganda.

Outside of our classrooms with Jjaja and Regina

Distributing food to our neediest families

Grand opening of Cathie Lee Nursery School

Teaching our kiddies how to play in a sand pit

Erecting our new sign on our road directing people to our ministry

23. JOVINS

When I first met Jovins, to be honest and to my shame, I saw her as a slight irritation. This lady kept coming to us day after day asking for work and at that stage, we had none to give her. We had only started the transition to the village from the city of Kampala. What I could do was to sit with her and hear her story. Robinah was my translator and thank goodness she knew enough of her dialect so we could communicate.

Jovins was a lady somewhere in her fifties or sixties. She was born deep in a village near the main town of Mbarara. She was one of five children and never attended school because in her family girls did not go to school. She looked after the family's cows. Her father was a hard man and he regularly beat Jovins, so of course she looked for the love she so craved elsewhere.

A much older man in his fifties took an interest in her and observing how she was being treated coerced her to come and live with him so he could take care of her. She left her home as a very young teenager and went straight into another terrible situation.

She bore three children to the man before she was 20 years old and lived a hard life struggling for the basics needed to care for the children. Through sheer determination and hard work two of her children had a primary education.

Eventually Jovins left a very hard situation and went to see her parents. Her father had died so she ended up staying with her lame mother to care for her. She eventually met Robert, who brought her to Kaliro Katono, abandoning her and leaving her destitute. That's when we met her and welcomed her in to our ministry.

Jovins would do the jobs that no one else wanted to do and showed her faithfulness to us. Robinah offered her a job looking after our pigs and so she was able to rent a small room to live in and buy food to eat.

Being a part of THM has made such a difference in Jovins life, giving her much hope and a wonderful smile on her face. She knows she is not forgotten and she believes that one day she will sleep in a house with electricity and her family will know the glory of God!

Jovins gives me a present before I leave to go back to Australia

24. TEACHER AZIDAH AND OUR LOYAL STAFF

We needed to find the right Head Teacher and staff for the nursery school so we started to put the word out. I knew we had to probably get someone from Kampala who could speak and teach in English as this could be hard to find from the village. People simply are not fluent English speakers even though English is Uganda's national language and all schools are supposed to teach in English.

So, we started to interview some different teachers we were put in touch with, knowing that we would be led to the right one at the right time if we were patient. Soon we were contacted by a lady named Azidah. On the recommendation of a friend we met with her.

Azidah was a lady in her thirties who had 10 years' experience as a teacher and a Head Teacher. She was working but was wanting to explore other opportunities. I liked her humility and maturity straight away and her ability to speak and understand English, and to understand what we were looking for in a Teacher. This position would be for a very motivated person to work as the supervisor and Teacher of over 20 three and four-year-old children with the help of two

Aides. They would be following the Ugandan curriculum and really heading up the whole school in its infancy. I had a good feeling about this woman and we agreed to pray about the employment and to meet together again. For Azidah it would mean relocating her life out to the village and away from the life as she knew it in the city of Kampala.

We were aware of another issue that Azidah needed to discuss with us first and we were allowing her the opportunity to tell us before a decision was made. Sure enough we received a call from her asking for another meeting. Azidah told us in her quiet way that she was expecting a baby. She had a boyfriend who was at that time standing by her even though he was younger and did not live with her. They were intending to marry in the future.

Azidah had a Muslim background but had become a Christian, as was her partner. She thought that because she was pregnant before marriage that we would judge her and certainly not give her this chance. It was a hard meeting for her as she thought, 'there goes my opportunity for this job'. We were impressed and thankful that she had told the truth and after talking about God's merciful love and second chances that He gives to us. As He led, we decided that Azidah was the right person for this position in this ministry. The baby was due in the school holidays and we would work it out from there.

A lot of Ugandan women have no choice but to have their babies and continue working to earn an income to live. It is a choice that they don't have because there are no government benefit supports. Family is their only support at this time and not everyone is living near family members or has a spouse to help them, as was in Azidah's case.

What better way to show Christ's love than to help this woman through this time in her life, giving her hope for her future.

Azidah moved out to the village into a small room that we rented for her as included in her trial contract for three months. She was perfect from day one of opening and showed her skill and dedication as the days went on.

We employed two young girls both around seventeen years old as helpers. One for cooking breakfast and lunch for the children and staff and the other as a Teacher Aide working with the children. This was a wonderful opportunity for these girls who were part of our ministry already.

Delilah was a local girl born in the district to a man with other wives and children, so she was given to her paternal grandmother around two months of age to raise. Fortunately, her father continued to care about her needs and she was sent to school for a primary education. The first time Delilah saw her mother was when she was seventeen years old. She didn't have the opportunity to continue her education and her dream of becoming a nurse faded over the years.

When we came to Kaliro Katono, Delilah signed up for the English and sewing lessons that we were offering. Living with her grandmother she did all the household duties as well as digging in the garden and growing their food. She quickly became a very active member of Harvest Church and joined the singing and dancing group. She was one of the best students in my English class and a very moral and well brought up young lady. So we knew that it was only a natural choice to offer her a position in our school.

Delilah became the Cook/Aide for Cathie Lee Nursery School alongside seventeen-year-old Favour.

Favour spoke English extremely well and was a delightful girl. She lived with her mother who broke rocks up in a quarry for a living. There were other children younger than Favour so she was required to look after them. Favour had been fellowshipping with us for a couple of years when she became pregnant. On my return to Uganda before opening the school Favour turned up to see me with a little baby bundle. She was scared and embarrassed to tell me as she knew that this had been an unfortunate moment in her life which resulted in her not being able to continue schooling as well as facing the wrath of her mother and other family members. We continued to support Favour as we were able to and when the position came up for the school, she also was a decision we made to try to help stop the cycle from continuing in her life.

As long as we can continue making a difference in one person's life then Treasure Harvest Ministries is working!

Julius is another wonderful life that's being changed. Julie, as he is fondly called many times throughout the day, is our Askari or security guard. He was born in West Uganda to Catholic parents one of four children, but tragically two of the girls died in their infancy. Julius and his brother Didas lived with their mum and dad until their parents separated when Julius was eight years old. He was raised by his mum who struggled to pay his school fees but fortunately a good Samaritan helped along the way to keep him in school in return for him looking after his cows when the school day had finished. This kind man passed away when Julius was thirteen and his schooling came to an abrupt halt. He continued to work with cows until he was twenty and moved away to look for a better paying job.

It just so happened that Julius met our Askari, Phillipo, who was moving away and looking for the right replacement for us at that time. Phillipo brought him along to meet Robinah and we hired him and have not looked back. He has been a loyal and reliable friend to us and we are happy to have him on the team.

Unfortunately, that hasn't always been the case as happens when working with people. In the early days we had employed a guard when we started ministry in Kampala. He was a loyal worker and helped out in many areas of the ministry even translating for us when we were invited to speak at different functions. What wasn't apparent was the hidden motives he had for working with us until God exposed them. We were forced to terminate all association with him because of the ministry even though we still had hearts of love and forgiveness toward him. That was an extremely hard time for us but we thank God for uncovering truth in what was being hidden, that it was brought to light, and for the strength to make the hard decisions and the growth that came afterward, even though it was a tragic situation at the time.

Julius our guard, always smiling

Finished ministry house referred to as The White House by the villagers

Our school kiddies learning about our fruit, grown on site

Harvest Church and community centre

Children out for a game at school

Full classroom at Cathie Lee School

25. SISTERLY WISDOM

Over the years I have had many meaningful and deep conversations with Robinah which have helped me find so much meaning to the world around me.

Once we were talking about compassion and she shared an African proverb with me.

'Wood on the fire becomes charcoal. Charcoal is not scared of the fire because it has already been in the fire'; which translates 'what doesn't kill you only makes you stronger'.

She went on to tell me about a lady called Josephine and her son. Josephine was a Ugandan lady, widowed with five children. When her firstborn son had grown up, he decided to go to South Africa to get work so he could help his family. He found work cleaning a compound and because he was a faithful man and diligent in his work, he was promoted to a secretary in his bosses' business. The boss left extra money lying around as a test but Josephine's son would always take the extra money to his employer. Because of his faithfulness and honesty, he was given an even higher position. The other South African workers became extremely jealous of this young Ugandan man and poisoned him. Tragically he died and his body was returned to his family in Uganda.

These stories are so frequently relayed to me and are part of life for many families here. Sometimes it almost seems as though it's expected. It can seem like we are talking about the weather. It's hard to get your head around the differences in the cultural ways of life living in a different place than where you were brought up, and it certainly gives you more compassion and empathy for people.

Treasure Ministries Dance Group performing for the community and for volunteer visitors

26. PERFECTING THE WALK OF A BAREFOOT PRIEST

Just before I was to return to Australia in 2019, we had organised an emerging leader's lunch after the church service one Sunday. We had about twelve people who had shown a desire to work with us and had the qualities we desired to train up as leaders in the ministry. So we had organised some local cooks to prepare a lovely lunch for us all to share. I remember my plate coming in first followed by the other plates of food. We ate together and discussed the future of the ministry and shared ideas on how we could grow together.

I was due to fly out the following week and unfortunately, I had a bit of a cold. That evening I was feeling desperately unwell and by the next day unable to function in anyway as I was so ill. Robinah and her son David carried me to the car to get me to the nearest clinic in our Trading Centre. I was delirious by this time and was put in a local wheelchair and rushed into the clinic and taken straight to a hard bench in the intensive care room. I was laid on it and an intravenous saline needle was put into my arm to rehydrate me. Blood was taken from me and I was given an injection of something to help me not feel so ill.

The blood test came back positive for food poisoning and, when I was able to move, was shifted to a bare room with two single cots in it. I was laid on one with the saline solution still dripping into me. At one stage in my delirium, I opened my eyes and looked up at Robinah, who informed me that a huge rat was underneath my bed. I remember saying that I didn't care! I was just too sick. A few hours later I was able to go home with antibiotics to help me through the next days.

My recovery was difficult and slow. I was flying out in a couple of days and I needed to be well enough to get on the plane. The journey was to be a long one with three stops and changes of aircraft. It actually ended up with a fourth stop that wasn't scheduled, somewhere over the Middle East, for fuel we were told. I remember that flight being one of the most difficult flights I had ever done as usually I love my long-haul flights as I make my way from aircraft to aircraft through the mazes of those gigantic and confusing airports.

Sure enough on re-entry I was shuffled off to the Doctors and it was confirmed by two medical practitioners that indeed I had been poisoned!

The question was, had this been simply a bad mistake or was it done intentionally? But even more than this, was it a curse put on me by witchcraft or a wilful act by someone who had access to my food!

The sad truth is that not everyone is on the same team in life and bad things really do happen to good people. In the months that followed even more disastrous things were to happen.

Early one year in Australia I had just gotten back to my home from a wonderful visit with family. On my way to the beach one morning as I was positioning some cables up high, I was flung off a chair and landed hands first on a hard tiled floor. Excruciating pain seared through my wrist and I knew that something really bad had happened. I managed to get up and went into absolute, 'save my life at all costs' mode. I unlocked the front door and located my mobile phone and made a call to a friend who was close by, appealing to her to come quickly, before walking over to the couch where I lost consciousness. I also managed to call an ambulance and tell them my address.

The next thing I remember was someone standing over me speaking and helping me and then the ambulance officers arrived. They transported me to the hospital where emergency care was given to me for a badly broken wrist. Not only was it broken but needed to be manually manipulated before setting. I remember the drugs given to me before the manipulation and that the room was quite full of people, about five or six. As I lost consciousness once again, I felt I was in a tunnel talking to Robinah and that she had a message for the Doctor who was working on me. As I came around, I felt a heavy wet sensation on my arm and as I opened my eyes, I immediately told everyone in the room not to speak. I had a message for the Doctor from Pastor Robinah, that God loved him and knew him and wanted him to know how much He really loved him. I swivelled my head to the only young woman in the room and said this was also for her. I remember the incredulous looks on their faces and I know that the Doctor spoke to me but I relaxed and closed my eyes as I knew that I had obediently delivered the message that I had been given. Unfortunately, the operation had not been successful and I would need surgery but as I was wheeled from that room, I caught sight of the Doctor and as our eyes met, I knew in his heart that he had received the message I had given him.

I was wheeled to a room in a ward and asked to make a decision on whether I wanted a plate and screws put into my wrist when they operated. I was so high on pain killers that I was so relieved that my friend was with me ready to help make those decisions. No one had any idea when I would be operated on and I remember having a conversation with the man in the bed across from me who was being sent home with a broken leg to await a suitable time for his operation to fix it. Then a miracle happened, I was told that the surgery for the repair of my wrist would happen that very night.

I was released the next day to begin the long and difficult healing journey to regain use of my wrist.

27. ROYALTY IS MY IDENTITY, SERVANTHOOD IS MY ASSIGNMENT

Often people ask me what a typical day for me is living and working at Treasure Harvest Ministries in Uganda. Every day is different as there are differing programs and classes offered on that day and different needs arise each day. Here is what one day in my life might look like at Treasure Harvest Ministries-

Awaking early to the two Hornbill birds crashing into my window, I rise and quickly dress ready for my morning walk through the village. I greet Jjaja Regina and her family members on the dirt track as they head to their gardens complete with hoes, machetes and a big knife for cutting and slashing and digging. I continue and pass women and children sweeping their compounds, always calling out a greeting. I jump out of the way of the man flying along the path on his bicycle going to work and move over for the children fetching water in their jerrycans from the local water spring for the day. They are usually carrying these heavy plastic containers on their heads or bicycles if they are lucky enough to have one for this job. I walk on past a local government school with students already in attendance doing early morning chores.

When I return home, I have a quick breakfast and prepare for the day. Already the teachers and children have started to arrive and there are women lined up to see Pastor Robinah and myself with needs and problems they are having.

I have a class to teach this morning at school with the children and pass by and greet the sewing ladies as they arrive for their class. I remember that they have put their order in to me for some new material that I will purchase the next time I'm in Kampala. I have so much fun with the kids as I teach them and read a story with them and then take them out for a steaming cup of porridge for their breakfast and playtime.

Midmorning I notice there is a woman and a small crying child sitting and waiting under a tree to see Pastor Robinah and myself. Robinah translates that the woman's child is sick and she has no money to take her to a clinic for medical attention and there is no food to feed her three other children at home. We see her and we hear her. We make a decision to help her to get to a clinic with the child and give her money for transport and medicine.

We then jump in the car and head into the trading centre to get food and supplies for the school and for this family. We pass by the carpenter's shop to check on our order for the new tables for the school he is making and organise delivery of them.

When we return, dropping off the supplies for the school we continue on to where the woman has told us she lives. Eventually we find the small mud brick dwelling with three sickly little children dressed in rags waiting in the dirt for their mother to return. A neighbour is keeping an eye on the kids. We talk to the neighbour who confirms the desperate needs of the family. The woman arrives back from the clinic with her child and some medicine. We organise a plan for the family and will continue to monitor her situation and welcome her and the children to our skilling classes and church family.

Arriving back home for a quick lunch of fresh coleslaw, avocado and fruit, its then time for afternoon discipleship and bible study class. As we fellowship together a truck arrives with a load of sand and rocks and dumps them in two heaps ready for the building project, the new school kitchen. We need to pay the truck driver and I run to get his payment. I pass by all the neighbouring kids swinging on our sturdy swing set we had made for the school.

The pigs still need to be fed and the other animals need to be rounded up but I know that Julius and Robinah will be attending to this.

Other youth are arriving for an afternoon soccer game and some of the girls are playing a game of volleyball. The dance and drumming teacher have arrived and some other young people are practicing their dance that they will perform in the church service on the weekend.

The power has gone out and I'm hoping it will come back in time before it gets dark so we can have good light to cook by and play our board games tonight. I also need to fit in a bit of paperwork and planning for the next day's lesson. I remember that I have promised the older girls a lesson in feminine hygiene sometime this week, so that needs to be organised as well.

The sun sets quickly and we have to make sure everyone has gone home before darkness settles. The stars are brilliant and quietness settles in the bush. The day is over and I have a peace and know that God's got me.

Back in Uganda tension was rising as the government was starting to shut down schools and businesses and restrictions were being put into place as Covid 19 was sweeping through the world and becoming known as a pandemic.

Movement was being restricted so as to slow the infection rate and this in turn was leading to another crisis as people were not allowed to go to their work places i.e., gardens and small roadside businesses. This in turn led to their income being diminished and not being able to feed the family, so people were starving.

As schools shut down this led to lots and lots of children being at home with nothing to do. Eventually a lot of teen pregnancies resulted and babies being born to young girls who did not have the skills or means to look after them. This was one of the disasters resulting from the turn of events. Death had come to visit our village. So many people became sick and passed away from this disease and the people who usually came to classes at our ministry were no longer able to attend. We managed to set up small groups that they could come to for a shorter time and the children could still keep getting some sort of teaching and a meal at least.

I was in constant contact with Robinah who was doing her best to keep things afloat in the ministry. All through the period of time when the pandemic raged through the world Treasure Harvest Ministries didn't really suffer much at all but was an absolute light and blessing to all around.

Meanwhile back in Australia I was working and raising funds so our work could continue.

Early in 2021 I was experiencing a familiar longing in my soul. I couldn't go back to Africa because we still had an international travel ban in Australia so I decided to visit my family in NSW. While visiting with my sister she picked up a message I had missed and encouraged me to answer it.

And so, began a whirlwind romance with a man I didn't even know.

I was completely side-tracked and side swiped and after 11 days I had a ring on my finger and had made the commitment to marry this man. I believed that this man was genuine and truly loved me. As he organised everything, I was already gone. The 'me' that people knew was nowhere to be seen. I was completely swept up into the fairy-tale story that was unfolding before me. The wedding was beautiful and enjoyed by many but as soon as we were married that all changed. The honeymoon was not what I expected and his bizarre behaviour was starting to surface, leaving me confused and very hurt. Soon after I was hospitalised as a result of a severe pseudo seizure brought on by extreme stress. I was having panic attacks and anxiety, things I had never experienced before and just feeling like my life was being sucked out of me. When I was in the hospital, I had a lot of tests on my brain and was told that a large lesion had been found in my cerebellum, so was scheduled to have an MRI for further investigation.

While in the hospital I was confused by everyone's behaviour and continued to be totally manipulated by the man who had professed to be a loving and caring husband to me. I saw and talked with social workers and police who helped to make me aware of strategies that were being used to coerce me, which only made me not trust anyone. Eventually I had the MRI which revealed two tumours in my brain which would be monitored and I was released to go home. Our relationship continued to decline and I became more aware that he had a different agenda than what I was led to believe, until eventually there was a separation and complete cut-off from one another. It seemed that I had been completely deceived by this person who was out to look after his own needs and not to have a mutually respectful and God honouring relationship with me. I was absolutely devasted and I am absolutely certain that God intervened on my behalf, putting a stop to this plan.

This was one of the biggest trials in my life and possibly the most traumatic event I have had to overcome. I needed to stay close to Jesus and to focus everything I had within me just to get through each day. It was extremely important to have caring, encouraging and loving people around me at this time but also important to distance myself from any negativity or criticism. It is so necessary to have the right tribe around you in life as you journey along through the many challenging situations that come and will continue to arise, because one thing I know is this: that there will be trials in this life but we are overcomers in and through Him.

I live to testify to the healing work of Jesus Christ in my life. He has totally healed me from that traumatic time and I am well today.

Reinhard Bonnke said

"Evangelism is a fiery chariot with a burning messenger, preaching a blazing Gospel on wheels of fire. Allow the Holy Spirit to make your life His chariot!"

During the pandemic in the years where I wasn't able to travel to Africa, God was at work. Initially people were forced to do things that were foreign to their way of life in the bush in rural Uganda. But eventually it was a case of the weeds being uprooted from the flowers and people began to really look at their lives and the way they were living and the things they were believing in.

We saw a shift in people's hearts to really go after truth and Harvest Church began to grow, at first slowly, but then in many, many hearts which were being challenged and changed, and the church overflowing with people. The dynamics were changing and all sorts of people started arriving in fancy cars and from other areas, not just locals.

We stepped up the fellowship groups and Robinah became a district leader of pastors and new connections and contacts were made with leading pastors in Uganda, some even by divine connections I had made while in Australia.

We managed to have some of our poorest most vulnerable children in our school sponsored by Australians who did a wonderful faithful job in their commitment to these kids.

Our school had an influx of children and we became a primary school as well, renaming it Cathie Lee Kindergarten and Primary School. We now have four classes, just under one hundred students and we intend to add more grades each year. Early in the morning we also pick up some of the students who don't live within walking distance. We have had to increase staff for the school. It can be a challenge to pay their salaries but we continue to walk in faith doing what we can and praying God will supply the rest.

One of our precious families lost their house and possessions in a freak storm in our village and had to live in a makeshift pole and tarp dwelling for months with absolutely no hope of being able to rebuild.

Alice was a single mother and had five children living with her, one of whom was a student at Cathie Lee School and also one of our sponsored children. Robinah and I came up with a plan to help this family and through the generosity of open hearts to the gospel and just plain compassion we were able to build a new, strong, two room, brick house for

Alice and her children on the land Alice owned. Furthermore, the house was up and roofed in three weeks! Thankfully just before the rainy season began.

Through prayer and divine connections in Australia I have met and befriended people connected to ministry in Uganda and through them I have been able to connect Robinah with leading pastors in our district, which only serves to broaden the gospel outreach through unity among the followers of Jesus. This is when God commands a blessing and I see this happening more and more.

As I prepare to return to Africa there are plans to plant our first medical facility on site, a malaria clinic. This will service all our school students, their families, staff, church and the community. Our nurse from Australia, Michele will also do a thorough medical check on all of our students.

It is an absolute privilege and such a wonderful blessing in my life to be able to serve my Lord Jesus Christ in this capacity He has given to me. In all my failures and flaws and utter dependency on Him to direct my steps, as I humble myself under His mighty hand and lay down my life to pick up His cross, I truly say, "Here I am Lord, send me and keep sending me!".

For to me to live is Christ and to die is gain.

End note

I will continue to serve in Uganda and this just might be 'to be continued...'

LESSONS I'VE LEARNT AS A WOMAN ON MISSION AND IN MINISTRY.

- When God impresses something on you, no matter how hard or big it may seem just set your mind and do it. He will move mountains for you but you have to step out in faith.
- Expect pushback in some form but be absolutely committed to the cause, push through and be resilient.
- Guard your heart above all things. Our hearts can deceive us so make sure you have wise council from people around you and be in God's word and right relationship with Him. Let Him fill those places in you that are vulnerable.
- Be prepared to be called on for the unexpected at any time and give it your best shot. You have everything you need, its already in you!
- Respond with love and care to people in emergencies. Use what you have and do more than is expected. You will reap respect, grateful hearts and may even change someone's whole life for better.
- You can't do it on your own. You need loyal people who are committed to the cause. Build a strong team of leaders and delegate jobs. Continually expose that team to learning and growing together.

- Learn to be patient. Somethings will take a long time to achieve especially when ministering in a foreign country. There is just a different way of doing things there, not wrong just different.
- Just keep going. Don't give up even when it looks hopeless. There will always be a way. For every problem there is a solution.
- If you are tired, rest. There is a time to act and a time to be still. Bad decisions can be made in haste.
- Don't miss opportunities. I believe in divine opportunities and appointments. Network with other likeminded organisations and people. Everyone has something to offer.
- Beware not everyone has your best interests at heart. People can have another agenda for wanting to work in your ministry or organisation. Watch and be patient. Behaviours and truth will eventually come out.
- Ministry is sacrifice. You will be uncomfortable and have to bear things that you wouldn't normally have to.
- Laugh a lot and learn to have fun every day. Things can get difficult and lonely especially in another culture when you are the only foreigner around.
- Remember He that is in you is greater than any obstacle you will come up against. Pray and trust God. He will come through for you but sometimes it won't be the way you thought it would be. Trust Him anyway. He could be saving you from something worse.
- Relax, you've got this. You are capable. Your unique gifts and abilities bring something beautiful and fresh in a very unique way.

- Learn to go without. Electricity, food, hot water, toilets, hair conditioner, whatever it is. You will survive. What doesn't kill you only makes you stronger.
- Be ready to minister to all sorts of people on the back of motorbikes, in slums, in jails, on the radio, to witchdoctors, to all people God puts in your path. Everybody needs Gods love and grace. Do it scared if you have to just do it!
- Be ready to humble yourself in situations especially if you are a guest in a foreign country. It's always a good idea to have a trusted interpreter with you.
- Sometimes things aren't going to work out the way you thought. Sometimes you will be wrong. Be brave enough to reconsider, apologise, forgive or whatever you have to do and learn from the experience. Don't give up, keep going. People need you.
- Love is more powerful than anything. Loving people enough to want to help change their lives for better is a good and noble thing. Love prevails over evil.
- Everything I have done and continue to do is a journey of faith. Sometimes I have no idea how I am going to achieve the next thing but I continue to take small steps in faith trusting God that He will make a way where there seems to be no way. I use what I have and He does the rest. I look back and realise He has always taken care of me and I know that He always will.

TREASURE HARVEST MINISTRIES

Our ministry is located in Kaliro Katono, near Kampala, in Uganda.

Treasure Harvest Ministries is serving in the following areas:

EMPOWERING – SKILLS-TEACHING
- Childcare/Education
- Christian education
- Skills for employment
- Equipping for business
- Agriculture
- Health/Hygiene
- Nutrition

BRINGING HOPE – GOSPEL OF JESUS
- Harvest Church
- Hosting conferences and events
- Leading people to Christ
- Bible Study groups
- Evangelism
- Baptisms
- Providing Bibles

LOVING PEOPLE – CHANGING LIVES
- Medical Clinics
- Feeding the hungry
- Clothing people/basic needs
- Refuge from domestic violence
- Rehabilitation after trauma
- Humanitarian work
- Survival solutions

OUR VISION –
is to empower people through development so that they can make their own decisions, including having an opportunity to decide to receive Jesus Christ as their Lord and Saviour.

AN OPPORTUNITY TO HELP –
We welcome skilled voluntary workers and teams to visit us and share their expertise, especially in the areas of ministry mentioned.

DONATIONS AND SUPPORT: –
contact Lesa Tacon
Email: lesa-22@hotmail.com
Facebook: Treasure Harvest Ministries
Website: www.treasureharvestministries.com

www.ingramcontent.com/pod-product-compliance
Lightning Source LLC
Chambersburg PA
CBHW050315010526
44107CB00055B/2255